Bonhoeffer's Black Jesus

Bonhoeffer's Black Jesus

Harlem Renaissance Theology
and an Ethic of Resistance

Reggie L. Williams

BAYLOR UNIVERSITY PRESS

Cover Design by Andrew Brozyna, AJB Design, Inc.
Book Design by Diane Smith

The Library of Congress has catalogued the hardcover edition
as follows:

Library of Congress Cataloging-in-Publication Data

Williams, Reggie L., 1971–
Bonhoeffer's black Jesus : Harlem Renaissance theology and an
ethic of resistance / Reggie L. Williams.
196 pages cm
Includes bibliographical references and index.
ISBN 978-1-60258-804-2 (hardback : alk. paper)
1. Bonhoeffer, Dietrich, 1906–1945. 2. Black theology.
3. Harlem Renaissance—Influence. I. Title.
BX4827.B57W545 2014
230'.044092—dc23
2014010728

The paperback ISBN for this title is 978-1-60258-805-9.

Printed in the United States of America on acid-free paper with a
minimum of 30% post-consumer waste recycled content.

For my wife, Stacy, and our children, Darion and Simone.

For my dear mother; thank you for believing in me.

For Glen, my fiercest advocate.

CONTENTS

ACKNOWLEDGMENTS

When I was completing my master's degree in theology, I took a course with Dr. J. Alfred Smith, studying African American spirituality. Dr. Smith was the senior pastor of Allen Temple Baptist Church, a singularly important black Baptist church located in a low-income neighborhood in Oakland, California. Smith would often tell the class, "African American spirituality is a spirituality that was born and shaped in the heat of oppression and suffering." It included a tradition of Jesus that connected the dissonant strands of grief and hope in the experience of black people who trusted in God to make a way out of no way. "Blackness is a metaphor for suffering," he told us. "To know blackness is to be connected to the suffering, hope, and purpose of black people."

On a day when the class was embroiled in a particularly spirited discussion, a young African American male student told a personal story of a shocking interaction with a white Christian woman. The student recalled a time when he was in the military, serving as a guard at the front gate of a base in the United States when a middle-aged white woman approached the gate in her car. She immediately asked to speak to his superior. He obliged her odd request and called for his coworker, a higher-ranking guard, also a black man. When the woman demanded to see another higher-ranking supervisor, the two men realized that something strange was happening. They pressed her for photo identification and the reason for her visit. "I am a Christian," she protested, "and since Jesus is white, I don't have to answer to anyone who is not white." In their shock, the two black men indulged the woman's request and called for their base supervisor, another high-ranking black man. When he showed up, his race and his authority were discouragement enough for the woman to leave the base.

The student's story in Dr. Smith's class piqued my interest in digging deeper into the narrative of my own Christian experience with racialized interpretations of Jesus. I saw a connection between interpretations of Jesus and social expectations within communities of worship, and my interest in the way our understanding of Jesus shapes the moral lives of Christians grew. The racist white woman at the military base was an extreme example, but historically she is not alone in her assumptions about Jesus and race and in the correlation between her racialized Jesus and her interaction with people of color. The location of her racist Christian rant, at a military base, also connects with historical permutations of religion, race, and militarism in the West that have blended together to influence Christian identity and Christian conduct negatively.

After that class, Dr. Smith insisted that I pursue doctoral work. "If you don't do it," he said, "it would be a mistake!" So I took his advice and was fortified with a subject matter that I wanted to pursue. During the first year in my doctoral program, I studied Dietrich Bonhoeffer with my mentor, Dr. Glen H. Stassen, who highlighted the African American community in Harlem as influential for Bonhoeffer's theological development. I noticed that Bonhoeffer's time in Harlem corresponded with the Harlem Renaissance, and I found that he wrote often about his fascination with Harlem. My close friend Ron Sanders saw a connection between my interests in christological hermeneutics and Bonhoeffer's time in Harlem as a project that I should pursue, and with Ron's advice I began to investigate the impact of the Harlem Renaissance on Bonhoeffer's interpretation of Jesus.

My study of Bonhoeffer's time in Harlem has been made possible by a handful of people who have provided guidance and insight to my research. I am grateful to my friend and mentor Dr. Glen H.

Stassen for his personal time and attention during a critical stage of this research. Thank you to my friend Dr. J. Kameron Carter for incomparable insight and support. Thank you, Dr. Larry L. Rasmussen and Dr. Clifford Green, for reading manuscripts and offering important advice. Thank you, Dr. Emilie Townes and Dr. Traci West, for giving advice to me about perception when I was a student that has guided me in all of my research. I am also grateful to Dr. Stacey Floyd-Thomas and Dr. Juan M. Floyd-Thomas for inspiration and guidance at the very beginning of this research.

Yet this project was almost killed before it could gain momentum. The global recession resulted in a personal economic crisis for my family. But the Forum for Theological Explorationn (FTE) gave me a grant that kept the door open to complete the research. Not only did they provide needed income but participation with the FTE introduced me to a vibrant community of scholars who were a tremendous encouragement. Thank God for Sharon Watson Fluker and Matthew Williams, who also insisted that I spend time in Harlem and covered the cost of my research in New York when I did not know whether I would have money for rent or groceries.

Although I was awarded generous help from FTE to continue my research, my wife and I were in need of financial assistance to carry us for a few months until the grant began. Friends and family came to our aid and covered the gap. They paid our rent, kept our lights on, and paid for our groceries to carry my family through the earliest stages of this research when my wife and I were jobless. I want to name them here to say thank you, again: Myrna Stephens, Christie and Jason Tarman, Kym and Dominic Paszkeicz, Marti and Jonathan Wilson, Charles and Cecelia Smalls, Carmen C. Lindsay, Dr. J. Alfred Smith, Pastor Stanley B. Long and South Bay Community Church, Pastor Kerwin Manning and Pasadena Church, and Pasadena First Baptist Church. For your love and support, we are forever grateful. God's grace was manifest in your largess at a difficult time in the life of my family.

I have additionally been fortunate to have other generous friends and colleagues who were an encouragement and who gave of their time and energy to assist me in numerous ways. I am grateful to Baylor University Press for the agreement to publish my manuscript. Thank you, Dr. Carey Newman, director of Baylor University Press, who saw its value and placed it in the publication process. Dr. Gladys Lewis has worked through every word of this manuscript in detail. She has been an invaluable gift. Thank you for sharing late nights and long days of editorial work online. Thank you William Otis and Nancy Lively, my extended family, for your invaluable help with the index. Thank you, Dr. Kevin McGruder, assistant professor of history at Antioch College and former archivist at Abyssinian Baptist Church, for your time and energy helping navigate sermon archives. Thank you, Reverend Dr. Calvin O. Butts, senior pastor at Abyssinian Baptist Church, for your generosity and support. Thank you, Michelle Wolff, for reading and offering valuable insight. Thank you to colleagues in the Christian Scholars Group, to friends and colleagues in the International Dietrich Bonhoeffer Society, and to my wonderful colleagues at McCormick Theological Seminary for valuable input in addition to giving me the time that I needed to finish this manuscript.

While writing this book, I have also had the pleasure of befriending the family of the African American man who introduced Dietrich Bonhoeffer to Abyssinian Baptist Church and to Harlem. In Bonhoeffer scholarship, he is commonly referred to as Frank Fisher, but in conversation with Fisher's niece, Dr. Minnie-Rose Richardson, and his daughters, Dr. Valerie Fisher and Judy Arrington, I was informed that no one among his family members or friends referred to him as Frank. To them, he was Albert or Al. His full birth name was Albert Franklin Owen Fisher, but he went by the name Albert Franklin Fisher. In honor of his family, I refer to him in this book as Albert or Al.

In my experience, community is vital for growth and survival. In many ways the community I shared in class with Dr. J. Alfred Smith helped me put together the dissonant strands of my own theological studies in a manner that propelled me toward a future in the academy. For that I am tremendously thankful. The community of my family, friends, fellow students, and colleagues is invaluable. You are why this work was possible.

INTRODUCTION

Dietrich Bonhoeffer championed a radical interpretation of Jesus and ethics that was validated by his resistance to the Nazis and his execution by them. He cultivated his ethical core, which led to his death, out of his fervent desire to encounter a meaningful and truthful experience with Christian theology in the person of Jesus. That understanding and relationship developed from his year of study in New York City when he encountered the black Christ who suffered with African Americans in a white supremacist world. He took that identity of the black Christ with him when he returned to Nazi Germany. To most pastors involved in Germany's Confessing Church resistance against the Nazi-sympathizing *Deutsche-Christens*, the German Christians movement, Dietrich Bonhoeffer was young, brilliant, and far too radical.[1] Well before the overtly racist Nazi government in Germany initiated World War II, opened concentration camps, and mobilized *Einsatzgruppen* (mobile death squads) throughout Europe to kill six million innocent people whom they declared *Untermenschen* (subhuman), Bonhoeffer was unique in his insistence that Christians in Germany publicly and adamantly oppose Nazi race hatred. Only when it was too late to stop the juggernaut of evil that the Nazis

1

became did his Christian colleagues in Germany realize that the
radical Bonhoeffer was right. Well-educated pastors and theologians who understood themselves to be faithful Christians, loyal
to family, church, and nation, became either silent bystanders or
active participants in Nazi atrocities and completely missed what
their professed faith in Christ required of them at that most crucial
moment in world history. Martin Niemöller's famous words after
World War II are displayed on the wall at the exit of the Holocaust
Museum in Washington, D.C., as testament to how he missed the
real Nazi threat even as a participant in the church resistance with
Bonhoeffer:

> First they came for the Socialists, and I did not speak out—
> Because I was not a Socialist.
> Then they came for the Trade Unionists, and I did not speak out—
> Because I was not a Trade Unionist.
> Then they came for the Jews, and I did not speak out—
> Because I was not a Jew.
> Then they came for me—and there was no one left to speak for me.

The fact that well-meaning, intelligent Christians in Germany did
not recognize the danger posed by the Nazis leaves one to wonder
how the young Bonhoeffer, born, raised, and trained in theology
with them, came to such a clear understanding of the problem
so early, when the majority of his associates were fundamentally
oblivious.

Bonhoeffer encountered the Christianity that animated the civil
rights movement years before it occurred, in New York's Harlem
community. When he was a Sloane Fellow at Union Theological
Seminary, Bonhoeffer became a student of the Harlem Renaissance
literary movement and was involved in one of America's foremost
black Baptist churches, Abyssinian Baptist Church, under the leadership of a prominent African American pastor, Adam Clayton
Powell Sr. The Christianity of the Harlem Renaissance was a
theological manifestation, post–Civil War, pre–civil rights movement, that identified Jesus with the oppressed rather than with the
oppressors, in a critical interrogation of the notions of God and
humanity embedded within the modern imperialist union of race
and religion.

The opposition to Bonhoeffer's developed Christian concern
for socially marginalized people included many of his own fellow

Christians in Germany. Although the pro-Nazi Christians of the German Christian movement and his colleagues in the Confessing Church movement understood themselves to be faithful Christians, Bonhoeffer identified lethal problems within their Christianity. Like American prosegregation Christians, the pro-Nazi German Christians demonstrated in a negative way that the mere claim to be a Christian is not an indication of faithful discipleship; what matters is one's interpretation of Christlikeness, how one interprets the way of Jesus. Bonhoeffer had formative experiences in New York in a key historical moment that inspired his efforts in Germany to uncouple the false connection between white imperialist identity and Jesus and its tragic imprint for Christianity. That struggle would last Bonhoeffer the rest of his life.

JESUS AND CHRISTIAN ETHICS

Much work in recent years has pressed the need to pay attention to the way of Jesus in Christian ethics. Christians must have a hermeneutic of Jesus to guide everyday Christian life within the community of believers who are committed to the gospel as a narrative that shapes Christian character. Bonhoeffer's experience in Harlem demonstrates that a Christian interpretation of the way of Jesus must be connected to justice for a Christian to see beyond primary loyalties to self and kind, to recognize the needs for justice in another's context, and to "love neighbor as self." The social connection that Bonhoeffer demonstrates can be described by values that give priority to the intrinsically vulnerable, fluid, and relational character of the gospel over and against the analytical, evaluative, and domineering Christianity of empire and colony.[2]

The language of empathy can also describe this social connection. Empathy suggests the ability to share in the experience of other people, to enter their context with the ability to reflect on the concrete needs for justice there without losing grasp on one's own separate identity.[3] This empathy is described as a prosocial, inductive encounter with others.

Yet an emphasis on empathy must include awareness of its potential abuses. Abusive empathy is prone to projection, in which the dominant, self-determining, autonomous persons within the social hierarchy bounce their image off the fungible body of fixed, commodified human subjects, only to see their own reflection returned to them. Empathy can be distorted to make it another way of keeping the subject in subjection, requiring an imagined white body overlaying a black one to humanize it.[4] Abusive empathy is that of a perceived superior, autonomous social identity imagining itself again by projecting itself against an inferior, dependent subject. It would be difficult to claim that empathy was a healthy component of Bonhoeffer's transformative experiences in Harlem if he did not learn something completely new. But his new learning in Harlem is apparent when consideration is given to at least a few key specifics: his frame of mind prior to coming to New York, the open vulnerability with which he encountered the Harlem community, and his post–New York turn toward the Jesus embraced by suffering African Americans, who suffers with them against systemic injustice and racial violence. Harlem became a part of Bonhoeffer's still-forming theological identity where he saw and valued the lives and experiences of real others, which indicates that the language of empathy and the language of intimacy and joining in Bonhoeffer's Harlem experience are healthy and appropriate descriptions of what happened there for him.[5]

In Harlem, Bonhoeffer practiced openness to inevitable revisions in his evaluation of himself and others.[6] His description of Jesus as *Stellvertretung* (empathic, vicarious representation) remained consistent throughout his career, which explains why the empathic encounter with others was already the framework of his Christology.[7]

Christ is the vicarious representative before God, the empathic representative who becomes a model of Christian discipleship by demonstrating the interaction that Christians are to have with one another.[8] As the vicarious, empathic representative, Christ is the reality that shapes the believer's existence in the world, and he models the incarnational being with and being for one another of Christian social interaction, in the concreteness of real life. In those encounters, Christians must enter their neighbor's context with a view to know their burdens and joys as Christians know their own.

Bonhoeffer's formation can be traced to his experiences in Harlem as a confrontation with his childhood and academic life in Germany by friendship with Albert Franklin Fisher, his African American friend who introduced him to Harlem, and three others who shared his quest for meaningful Christianity. He became aware of the way that Western Christianity is calibrated to a harmful ideal by a false connection between imperialism and Christianity. Experiences of spiritual growth in Harlem gave Bonhoeffer a healthier encounter with Jesus by way of a connection between Jesus and suffering within an ethic of resistance that identifies Jesus with the oppressed, rather than the oppressors. A principal site for the practice of his new understanding of Christ, the black Christ, took place in the Harlem Renaissance and in worship at Abyssinian Baptist Church, where he learned more about a tradition of Jesus in an ecclesial community that stressed attention to concrete historical realities and demonstrated a model for *Stellvertretung* as the harmony of all of life under the gospel. Bonhoeffer returned to Germany with key developments in his faith that gave him the ability to see singular distortions in German Christianity and empowered him to push back against the emerging Nazi government racism.

Bonhoeffer's imprisonment at Flossenbürg concentration camp and his execution on April 9, 1945, was the inevitable result of more than the hatred that killed more than six million Jews, gypsies, homosexuals, and handicapped persons within Hitler's Nazi regime; Bonhoeffer was also brought to that moment by Christian complicity and apathy. In addition, he was compelled to be there by the Christ he saw hidden in suffering. His commitment to embrace Christ left him with no other choice in a society where indifference replaced concern for the cries for help from the margins. In Harlem, that was the black Christ, despised and lynched time and again by white racist Christians, and in Germany Jesus was sent to Nazi gallows and gas chambers. Christians in Germany failed to hear Bonhoeffer's early warnings; they did not understand the dangers he was pointing out to them. They simply were not equipped with the same perceptive insight. But Bonhoeffer would not have seen the danger so clearly either, and he may have avoided his fate at Flossenbürg that Monday morning in April, in solidarity with Christ, if it were not for his experience in the Harlem Renaissance that validated the cosufferer image in human practice as he learned to act on behalf of the hungry, the poor, and the downtrodden, marginalized members of every human context.

CHAPTER ONE

TO HARLEM AND BACK
Seeing Jesus with New Eyes

Disaster can lead to transcendence, but the journey between the two may require time and suffering. Dietrich Bonhoeffer's *via dolorosa* took him from the loss and despair of World War I to Gestapo martyrdom and a crown of glory. World War I was a catastrophe for Germany. Its aftermath left Germany sifting through the rubble of shame and suffering, trying to salvage the remnants of its past. The injuries that the war inflicted on Dietrich Bonhoeffer's boyhood psyche remained sensitive twelve years later, as evidenced by the stories he shared about that terrible time. Bonhoeffer was a twenty-four-year-old postdoctoral student, studying for one year, 1930–1931, as a Sloane Fellow at Union Theological Seminary in New York, during a time of transition in Germany. But New York was a broader classroom than the spaces for learning provided by the seminary. In New York, Bonhoeffer was wrestling with the aftermath of the terrible war for his country while struggling to imagine himself as a pastor and theologian in a newly emerging Germany. The postwar world was in the grips of the global Great Depression, and Bonhoeffer was an unsettled, gifted young German student, looking in New York for a theological identity.

His search took him to numerous churches in America during his fellowship year. Many of his church visits included speaking to congregations or to student groups about the impact of World War I on his home country. On some occasions, he spoke candidly about the war's toll on his own family:

> Two brothers of mine stood on the front. The older one 18 years old was wounded, the younger one 17 years old was killed. Three first cousins of mine were also killed . . . although I was then a small boy, I never can forget those most gloomy days of the war. Death stood for the door of almost every house and called for entrance.[1]

He described Germany as a nation transformed from an idyllic family into a house of mourning.[2] And though Germans welcomed the end of the horrors that accompany war, after World War I Germany saw no end to the story of suffering; it was but a different chapter.[3]

BONHOEFFER'S CHILDHOOD

In the years prior to World War I, things were much different for Bonhoeffer. He was the product of a large, close-knit family of eight children that prized the characteristically German virtues of diligence, excellence, and achievement.[4] In spite of Bonhoeffer's chosen career as a theologian, the Bonhoeffers were not a church-going family. They knew the Christianity of the German cultured upper class, with its music, poetry, literature and hymnody, and Bible. The Bonhoeffers prayed, sang, and read the Bible at home.[5]

Everything changed in Germany with the arrival of World War I. The death of Bonhoeffer's brother Walter and the intensity of his mother's corresponding grief were key war wounds that altered the course of his life.[6] Two years after Walter was killed, fourteen-year-old Dietrich knew exactly what career path he wanted to take.[7] While he was an undergraduate, in a brief autobiographical statement, Bonhoeffer wrote, "From the time that I was thirteen years old it was clear to me that I would study theology."[8] Bonhoeffer's theological prescience was conceived in the wounds of war.

As a theology student, Bonhoeffer was aware that he was brilliant. He was motivated to acquire as much knowledge as he could, as quickly as possible, to demonstrate his abilities. Because of his confidence and zeal, Bonhoeffer was not interested in being under the direct guidance of a master; he sought to make his own way.[9]

As a graduate student, Bonhoeffer crafted a unique social theology by synthesizing two opposing schools of thought; he combined the work of three particularly influential like-minded liberal scholars from the University of Berlin, Karl Holl, Reinhold Seeberg, and Adolf von Harnack, with the newly emerging dialectical theology of Karl Barth.

The three Berlin theologians constituted a Berlin tradition of old guard liberal theology, with each member contributing from his respective discipline.[10] Holl was responsible for inspiring a "Luther Renaissance" in 1910 with a public lecture and the subsequent publication of a series of essays on the great German reformer. Holl revived Martin Luther's famous slogan, *sola gratia, sola fide* (by grace and faith alone) and combined it with Luther's insistence that "justification is God's gift and promise through the church."[11] Holl's reference to justification encountered by grace as a gift from God through the church left its mark on Bonhoeffer.

Studies with Seeberg gave Bonhoeffer the theological language of sociality that described "Christ existing as church-community."[12] Seeberg helped Bonhoeffer to see Jesus as the initiator of a new humanity that identified Christ with the community of the church in the world, as the location where the Holy Spirit becomes flesh. Adolf von Harnack was a historical theologian and a neighborhood friend of the Bonhoeffer family. Harnack's work could be characterized as "liberal theology at its height," appropriating the term "liberal" positively, as its defenders used it.[13] Harnack argued for historical concreteness in order to free Christians from the trappings of religion to grasp the essence of faith, which he argued could be accessed by reason. By combining the work of Berlin's old guard with the work of Karl Barth, Bonhoeffer turned the dissonance of two diametrically opposed schools of thought into an innovative, Christ-centered harmony.[14]

Bonhoeffer harmonized Barth's insistence on the otherness of God with his Berlin professor's historically concrete, modern German theology to develop a theology of sociality that emphasized the revelation of God in the world, in the person of Jesus. For Bonhoeffer, Christ is present in the world as the church, in the communion of saints, in the community of believers. Christ existing as the church is empathic, vicarious representative action, or Jesus as *Stellvertretung*, who became *Kollektivperson*, or humanity combined in one, by standing in for all of humanity in the sin and shame that makes us hide and isolate ourselves from God and one another. Bonhoeffer's interpretation of Christ as vicarious representative action is not only who Jesus is; *Stellvertretung* as vicarious representative action is an ethical mandate for followers of Jesus.

Yet as a creative young theologian, Bonhoeffer remained sympathetic toward the German nationalism that was popular within the general mind-set of post–World War I Germany. His nationalist sympathies produced contradictions in his innovative theology at the early stages of its development. The Lutheranism of his professors in Berlin described theology as a function of the church only and kept intact the characteristically Lutheran two-kingdom split, which argued for a separation between the church and the government, insisting that each had its unique and separated realm of authority. In daily life, the two-kingdom split meant that Christian piety was a matter for one's private life, but in public the laws of the state guided Christians.

But the predominant expression of Christianity in postwar Germany was a malaise of Lutheranism, social Darwinism, and nationalism fused in a triumphalist view of history described as God's *orders of creation.*[15] Bonhoeffer's system was no exception to the norm; in his early years, his creative theology was seduced by the predominant expression of Christianity in Germany. The concept of orders became theological support for the Nazi language of blood and soil, of racial superiority, and of a pure *Volk.*[16] The presence of the orders in Bonhoeffer's early theology underscores overt contradictions in his developing theology, beginning with the dissonance between nationalism and ecumenism.

Nowhere are these contradictions more evident than in a set of lectures that Bonhoeffer delivered as an assistant pastor of an expatriate German congregation in Barcelona, Spain, in 1928–1929. He preached twenty sermons that year, but in the winter Bonhoeffer delivered three academic lectures for his congregation, of which the final two are most explicitly dissonant. These lectures reveal a discordant connection in Bonhoeffer's pre–New York theology between an ecumenical, Christ-centered faithfulness and a common loyalty to German *Volk*. On December 11, 1928, he delivered the second lecture, entitled "Jesus Christ and the Essence of Christianity." Bonhoeffer argued that Christ makes ethical claims on the lives of Christians:

> The religion of Christ is not the tidbit after the bread; it is the bread itself, or it is nothing. . . . Various attempts have been made to eliminate Christ from the contemporary life of the human spirit. . . . The only thing these attempts do not do is take him seriously. . . . They do not draw the center of their own lives into contact with Christ's claim to speak and indeed to be *the* revelation of God. . . . If there is something in Christ that makes claims upon my entire life, from top to bottom, and does so with the full seriousness of the realization that it is God who is speaking here, and if it is only in Christ that God's word once became a present reality, then Christ possesses for me not only merely relative but also absolutely urgent significance.[17]

For Bonhoeffer, Christianity centers totally on Jesus. The claim to Jesus' "urgent significance" implies the ethical imperative of Jesus the *Stellvertretung* as God's self-revealing presence in the church. Jesus as *Stellvertretung* makes him a guide for our social action, in addition to providing concrete interaction with Jesus, who is presently experienced within the communion of saints.

But Bonhoeffer's argument for the urgent significance of Christ and Christ's ethical imperative was missing critical substance. At this point in his theological career, Bonhoeffer did not refer to the Bible for Christian discipleship. As a result of that glaring omission, it was easy to blend the way of Jesus with German nationalism and to consider patriotism an element of Christian discipleship. With the Bible omitted as a source of concrete guidance for Christian moral living, the popular Lutheran language of the two kingdoms, replete with the nationalist notion of orders of creation, filled the void.

Speaking again to his expatriate congregation in Barcelona, Bonhoeffer's third lecture, entitled "Basic Questions of a Christian Ethic," emphasized German patriotic discipleship, with Bonhoeffer's emphasis on loyalty to the superior German peoples, or *Völker*:

> [*Völker*] are like individuals.[18] At first they are immature and need guidance. Then they grow into the blossom of youth, mature into adults, and they die. . . . Growth requires expansion; an increase in strength involves pushing aside other individuals.[19] In that respect the life of an individual person is no different than that of a people [*Volk*]. . . . Strength also comes from God and power and victory for

> God creates youth in individuals as well as in nations. . . . Should not
> a Volk experiencing God's call on its own life in its own youth and in
> its own strength, should not such a people be allowed to follow that
> call, even if it disregards the lives of other people? God is the Lord
> of history.[20]

The language of the Lord of history and of blood and soil carried
distinctive meaning within the context of German postwar shame
and longing. Hope for Germany's future included crafting a narrative on which to hang their current experiences to connect their
imperialist nostalgia with a vision of a brighter German tomor-
row. Longing for Germany's glorious past framed the story of a
recovered, victorious *Völker*.

That longing was a contradiction in Bonhoeffer's theology.
Jesus was central to Bonhoeffer's theology, as the revelation of
God in the world, which would imply a more global relevance
than his emphasis on German *Volk* would allow. Hence, the
story of a victorious, superior Germany and the gospel of Jesus
the *Stellvertretung* fit together awkwardly; they were tethered to
each other by nationalism that supplanted content from the gospel
and turned Jesus into a fetish of German cultural longing. The
implications of Bonhoeffer's pairing of Jesus and culture were
significant; Christians were virtually invisible in German society,
absorbed into the German culture of Protestantism, with its liberal
Christian language of human achievement and of nationalism. A
good Christian looked no different than a patriotic German, tethered firmly to *Volk*ish, or German-centered, loyalties.

THEOLOGIA CRUCIS OR THEOLOGIA GLORIAE

The *Volk*ish German Christian was the result of theology shaped
by an early longing for empire and triumph, rather than by what
Bonhoeffer would later value: the recognition of suffering. He
came to rebuke the theology that resulted in the invisible *Volk*ish
Christian as a misrepresentation of the Lutheran *theologia crucis*,
the "theology of the cross."[21] Luther contrasted the *theologia crucis* with a *theologia gloriae* to make the point that the revelation of
God occurred not in glory, or triumphalist comprehension of theological themes grasped once and for all, but in the mystery of God's
hiddenness, in suffering and shame. But popular interpretations of
Luther's *theologia crucis* emphasize hiddenness as the absence of

distinctively Christian behavior. The invisible Christian places an emphasis on God's redemptive act alone, not Christian behavior, by highlighting "hiddenness" in a sentence that reads "Christ *hidden* in suffering and shame," in support of a *Volki*sh two-kingdom split that advocated Christianity as a matter for one's private life only. For Luther, the result of a theology of glory was a Christian far too confident about facile theological responses to complex questions of life that have not been engaged faithfully. But the two kingdom's interpretation of the theology of glory passes over real life and concreteness, making room for Christian disciple-ship to be defined by popular social and political themes, rather than by obedience to Scripture and a concrete Christian ethics. This distinction becomes clear with a return to the lecture on the essence of Christianity. As Bonhoeffer continued the lecture, his latent description of *theologia crucis* reflected interpretations that emphasized the hiddenness of God. Accordingly, the hiddenness of God exposes the hubris of works of righteousness:

> When people merely listen, merely receive, that is, when they seem to be the farthest from God in irreligion and immorality, then God is closest to them. Religion and morality contain in them a germ of hubris, the essentially Greek concept of hostility toward the divine, the germ of pride, of arrogance.[22]

By listening and receiving rather than acting on Christ's social com-mands, believers can avoid the pride and arrogance that accompa-nies all religious claims to ethical positions. Indeed, Christianity does not guide us to behave in a particularly "Christian" way, as Bonhoeffer claimed, "the Christian message is basically amoral and irreligious, paradoxical as that may sound."[23] To drive home his point about *theologia gloriae*, in his third lecture Bonhoeffer insisted that "Christianity and ethics have absolutely nothing to do with each other. There is no Christian ethic. From the idea of Christianity, there is absolutely no transition to the idea of eth-ics."[24] Implicit in Bonhoeffer's argument is the claim that attempts to respond to Christ's commandments as if they were meant to be followed become *theologia gloriae*, or religious hubris. Rather, good religious performance, for the early Bonhoeffer, was confor-mity to Christ's "hiddenness" in the world, which included popu-lar German nostalgia for the advancement of the *Völker*. Jesus fit this German narrative by providing Christians with grace to help advance the hopes of a renewed German society, in full support of the German *Volk*.[25]

For the sake of the *Volk*, war could be justified,[26] murder could be sanctified;[27] Christ demands the maintenance of no laws except the law of freedom justified by grace.[28] This language used in reference to Christianity ran counter to the language of Christ as *Stellvertretung*. With this contradictory language, Bonhoeffer made use of the gospel for nationalism by avoiding the Bible. Yet, the pre–Sloane Fellowship Bonhoeffer did take notice of at least one of the contradictions in his developing theology. The direction of Bonhoeffer's interpretation of Luther's notion of the *theologia crucis* led him to an interpretation of Christ's suffering and death as behavior that demonstrated God's love.

Love, in addition to the law of freedom, becomes a principle that guides the Christian life. But love, like the Bible, makes limited claims upon Christian social behavior. Bonhoeffer asks, "Should we love our enemies as Christ commanded in the Sermon on the Mount?" He answers his question by explicitly betraying the synchronization of his early theology and popular German nationalism. In the third lecture on the basic questions of a Christian ethics, he claims that love of enemy over love of *Volk* is evil:

> It would be an utter perversion of one's ethical sensibilities to believe that my first duty is to love my enemy and precisely in so doing to surrender my neighbor to destruction, in the most concrete sense. It is simply not possible to love or, as the case may be, to protect both my enemy and my people [*Volk*]. . . . God gave me my mother, my people [*Volk*]. For what I have, I thank my people [*Volk*]; what I am, I am through my people [*Volk*], and so what I have should also belong to my people [*Volk*]; that is the divine order [orders of creation] of things, for God created the peoples [*Völker*].[29]

Bonhoeffer's Barcelona lectures reveal a Bonhoeffer who was in step with German nationalism. A Christian participation in war, when one's own *Volk* are in danger, permitted a suspension in the commandment to love a non-German neighbor. The empathic, socially vicarious language of *Stellvertretung* is modified, and German-centric nationalism, rather than Christ-centered ecumenism, becomes the guide to Bonhoeffer's Christianity. That was the case with Bonhoeffer's pre–New York theology, and it evidenced the presence of still-raw wounds from the war.

His German postwar interpretation of Christ existing as the church-community turned Jesus into God's endorsement of the retooled narrative of the *Volk*, a point that he demonstrated with unabashed clarity at the end of his second Barcelona lecture when he proclaimed, "German people, that is your God!"[30] His best friend and biographer, Eberhard Bethge, explained that it took further developments in his interpretation of the *theologia crucis* to save him from this thinking.[31]

NOT YET A CHRISTIAN

After his pastorate in Barcelona, Bonhoeffer spent a year writing his second dissertation. With it completed, he sensed that he had problems within his theology. Prior to his trip to New York, Bonhoeffer confessed his growing uneasiness with academic theology: "I feel in general that academic work will not hold me for long."[32] Bonhoeffer later recalled his pre–New York career and wrote, "I had not yet become a Christian but, wildly and undisciplined, was my own master. I know that at that time I took personal advantage of the cause of Christ and served my own vanity."[33] And he found neither his vanity nor his nationalism to be satisfying. His time as a pastor in Barcelona contributed to his growing dissatisfaction with academic theology and made it apparent to him that he did not see any representation of Christ existing as church-community within the culture Protestantism of German churches. In Germany, his desire for difference resulted in a theological and personal deadlock, which was for him a crisis at the beginning of his professional life.[34] Academic theology and pastoral ministry were both at odds with one another for Bonhoeffer yet at the same time disturbingly harmonious. Bonhoeffer could not find concrete responses to Germany's postwar social crises in the church or the academy; he found that both sources offered only popular contradictions and little genuine Christian guidance. Bonhoeffer was in this theological condition when he left Germany for America, still nursing his boyhood war wounds, in search of "a cloud of witnesses" to help solve his theological crisis.[35]

BONHOEFFER IN NEW YORK: THE QUEST FOR
"A CLOUD OF WITNESSES"

Union Theological Seminary's Sloane Fellowship provided annual funding for three European students to participate in a one-year residency program.[36] Typically Sloane Fellows would end their fellowship year having earned a master of arts degree in theology. Two other Sloane Fellows joined Bonhoeffer at Union that fall, Erwin Sutz from Switzerland and Jean Lasserre from France, and both had finished a master's degree by the end of their Sloane Fellowship year.[37] Clearly that would not be the case with Bonhoeffer. In the fall of 1930, the German Sloane Fellow resembled a master's student only in his age. At twenty-four years old, Bonhoeffer's academic accomplishments already included an appointment to the faculty at the University of Berlin, which was awaiting his return to Germany. He hardly needed more time in the theology classroom as a student to ensure a teaching career.

His exceptional drive for academic accomplishment explains some of his harsh criticism of the theology that he encountered in the classroom and among the students at Union. Bonhoeffer was brilliant and highly motivated. He was soon comparing his performance with that of the students and the faculty, and he claimed they were all operating at a subpar academic level and with a less-than-Christian theology. He found them hesitant to talk about Jesus, sin, and salvation, which for Bonhoeffer made their Christianity suspect. He was disdainful of theology in America during his first semester, and he was not quiet about it. His theological disapproval extended to his experience of white churches in New York as well, and he became scornfully derisive of the Christianity he experienced during his many congregational visits. Upon his arrival in New York, his search for a cloud of witnesses left him quickly disillusioned.

THE PROBLEM WITH WHITE AMERICAN
THEOLOGY

Bonhoeffer arrived in New York one year after the stock market crash that initiated the worldwide Great Depression. He disembarked onto American shores to meet scenes of hunger and despair that resembled postwar Germany. Ironically, the conditions that brought him to a theological deadlock in Germany had also followed him across the Atlantic, only to greet him on unfamiliar soil.

Not only did he find famine and economic strife but also academic and church theology in America continued to yield very little concrete insight for Christian living. The content of theology in America was different, making it difficult for him to see the broader implications of Christ as *Stellvertretung*. Rather than the dogmatic theology of Bonhoeffer's formative German theological environment, he found that in America "pragmatism [had] expelled dogmatics . . . and the question of truth [had] been supplanted by utility."[38] That difference communicated to Bonhoeffer that critical content from the gospel and about Christ was missing in the classroom and the pulpit. In an end-of-the-year report about his Sloane Fellowship prepared for the Church Federation in Germany after he returned home, Bonhoeffer wrote about students in practical theology seminars asking whether one really must preach about Christ.[39] He reported how students laughed at a passage from Luther's *Bondage of the Will* about sin and forgiveness that was shared during a public lecture.[40] Significant features of Bonhoeffer's academic training were mistreated, belittled, or completely missing in New York. By Christmas, Bonhoeffer had come to the conclusion that theology did not even exist at Union:

> There is no theology here. Although I am basically taking classes and lectures in dogmatics and philosophy of religion, the impression is overwhelmingly negative. They talk a blue streak without the slightest substantive foundation and with no evidence of any criteria. The students—on the average twenty-five to thirty years old—are completely clueless with respect to what dogmatics is really about. They are not familiar with even the most basic questions.[41]

Bonhoeffer's description of Union Seminary students as "clueless" extended to his commentary on the American version of liberal theology. The foundation of theology at Union was modern American liberalism, which Bonhoeffer saw as woefully inadequate at best or at worst heretical.[42] He held a proud interpretation of the place that the German academy had within the larger academic world, and he was certain that his community of modern liberal American students and faculty at Union was incapable of even comprehending theology from the German academy.[43]

THE PROBLEM WITH WHITE CHURCHES

The white churches that Bonhoeffer visited were plagued with the same theological problems that he found in the classroom at Union. He complained about the lack of content in the sermons he attended: "In New York, they preach about virtually everything; only one thing is not addressed, or is addressed so rarely that I have as yet been able to hear it, namely the gospel of Jesus Christ, the cross, sin and forgiveness, death and life."[44] Bonhoeffer concluded that the theological vacuum in New York's white congregations qualified them for a label different than church:

> In the place of the church as the congregation of believers in Christ, there stands the church as a social corporation. . . . Some churches are basically "charitable" churches; others have primarily a social identity. One cannot avoid the impression, however, that in both cases they have forgotten what the real point is.[45]

The missing "real point" was for Bonhoeffer a matter of urgency. "For the German observer," Bonhoeffer claimed, "the question becomes even more urgent about just how this particular form of the church and its distortion could have occurred."[46] But his disappointment with theology in the classroom, and in the pulpit, was not very different from the issues that sent him on his quest for a cloud of witnesses. He had similar Christian problems at home in Germany.

BONHOEFFER AND CIVILIZED AMERICAN CHRISTIANS

In America, instead of German nationalism parading as Christian discipleship, Bonhoeffer was grappling with modern theological liberalism in white American Christianity. Theological liberalism in America was optimistic about articulating a middle way between fundamentalism and atheism, reconceptualizing what might be considered traditional, or even fundamentalist, Christianity in light of the influence of modernity within the broader white American society.[47] Union was a citadel of white American modern liberal Christianity. The liberal theological worldview made Christianity into the apotheosis of human social progress, reducing the language of salvation and sin to religious relics in order to accommodate itself to a broader, modern public. At Union, the modern, civilizing temperament was the reason liberal white students laughed at Luther's reference to sin and forgiveness and questioned whether it was relevant to continue talking about Jesus.[48] White American liberals were motivated by an effort to cultivate and civilize what they understood as the naturally brutish faculties within the individual as well as society.[49] Liberal Christianity's civilizing scheme accommodated Christianity and American society, making little distinction between human achievement in modernity and industry and the civilizing virtues of Western Christian refinement.[50] For American liberal Christians, much the same as it was in Germany, Christianity, civilization, and culture were nearly synonymous.

The content in America was different and foreign, but the concept of Protestant culture was not. Consequently, Bonhoeffer found theology at Union and in white churches very disappointing; in his first experiences of America, he found no representation of Christ existing as church-community. If those theological encounters had been the sum of his experience with Christians in America, Bonhoeffer's hopes for an end to the deadlock and an encounter with a cloud of witnesses would have been dashed.

ENTERING THE CLOUD OF WITNESSES

To his credit, Bonhoeffer continued searching in spite of persistent disappointment. His search led him to Harlem, New York's African American community, where he was introduced to a tradition of Jesus that surprised him. That tradition became decisive for his continued theological development. In addition, his relationships with four close friends at Union, Americans Albert Fisher and Paul Lehmann and the other Sloane Fellows, Erwin Sutz and Jean Lasserre, provided positive content for what he described years later as having "the greatest significance" for him "up to the present day."[51]

Bonhoeffer's friendship with Lehmann and Sutz gave him the benefit of stimulating familiarity. Lehmann, Bonhoeffer's closest American friend and one of Union's Ph.D. students during Bonhoeffer's Sloane Fellowship, compared the German liberal theologian Albrecht Ritschl with Karl Barth in his dissertation.[52] Sutz had studied with Barth and would eventually arrange the first meeting between Barth and Bonhoeffer. Given Barth's strong influence on Bonhoeffer, Lehmann's and Sutz' theological interests created a common bond. Additionally, Lehmann was fond of Western Europe in general, while Sutz and Bonhoeffer were both accomplished pianists. Tying all of their commonalities together was the fact that the three men could converse fluently in German.[53]

ALBERT FRANKLIN FISHER

But the German language was not a connecting factor with Fisher and Lasserre. These friendships were tailor-made to jar his theology loose from its captivity to nationalism by inviting Bonhoeffer into empathic experiences that were troubling for them yet foreign to him, which enabled him to see broader implications of Jesus as *Stellvertretung*.[54]

Albert Fisher was born in Birmingham, Alabama, in 1908 into a highly educated African American family. He was the youngest of six children, the only boy, and an heir to a lineage of preachers that included his maternal grandfather, Anthony Richardson, who was born into slavery and yet as a slave learned to read.[55] After slavery, Richardson's literacy helped him to navigate the hostilities of white supremacy during the emergence of the Jim Crow laws that replaced slavery as a new racial organizing scheme. Richardson's grasp of the gospel as an African American in an overtly hostile, racist environment equipped him to preach the gospel as a means of resistance and survival.[56]

Albert Fisher knew his maternal grandfather. Indeed, Al Fisher knew that he came from a proud family lineage of educated black Baptist clergy on both sides of his family. His father, Charles Fisher, received his bachelor of arts degree from Leland College in Louisiana before earning a bachelor of divinity degree from the Baptist Union Theological Seminary.[57] Charles Fisher was pastor of the 16th Street Baptist Church in Birmingham, Alabama, during its construction in 1898, roughly sixty-five years before it was bombed by white racists, killing four young girls three weeks after Martin Luther King Jr. delivered his "I Have a Dream" speech.

Pastor Charles Fisher was no stranger to white racist terrorists threatening the lives of the children of his church. In 1914 members of his congregation made plans to take children from their church to visit the Birmingham zoo. When local whites caught wind of their plans and threatened violence in response to the children's visit, Fisher called off the outing for the safety of the children.[58] Like all African Americans in Jim Crow America, Pastor Fisher knew to take the threat of white violence seriously.

Fisher's 16th Street Baptist Church was the center of Birmingham's black community. In addition to providing a place of worship, Pastor Fisher was politically active, supporting the African American community by protesting against humiliating Jim Crow laws as a vocal advocate for racial justice. The church also had a social service association that provided numerous forms of aid to black workers, including a kindergarten for small children and a community extension of the church, with financial assistance programs.[59]

In 1930 Charles Fisher left Birmingham for Selma, Alabama, to become the dean of the School of Theology of Selma University and a professor of languages. Also in 1930, Dean Fisher's son, Albert, joined Dietrich Bonhoeffer with other new students at Union Seminary in New York.

Albert Fisher was born in the segregated south, but his move to Union was not his first encounter with integrated education. During his childhood, Fisher attended elementary school in Hartford, Connecticut.[60] Like many blacks in Jim Crow America, Fisher's family was accustomed to negotiating the dangers within a white American society, where the white majority vacillated between a malignant apathy, on the one hand, and bitter acrimony, on the other, toward black people. Hartford in America's less-violent northern states was part of the Fishers' process of negotiating violent white supremacy, as were theological education and church ministry. Fisher's family experience of Christianity in America indicated that navigating the poles of fundamentalism and liberal modernity were not the only challenges facing the gospel in America. Most liberal whites failed to see white supremacy as a matter for Christian attention, and as a consequence they ignored the constant dangers of daily life in America for black people. But avoiding racism was not a choice for African American Christians; it was a matter of life or death in a society organized by race and enforced by violence. Consequently, Bonhoeffer's friendship with Albert Fisher introduced him to Christian worship with an inherently different view of society. With Fisher, Bonhoeffer encountered Christians aware of human suffering and accustomed to living with the threat of death in a society organized by violent white supremacy.

The threat of death was constant and real, as evidence showed. According to conservative estimates, more than 4,700 lynchings occurred in the United States between the early 1880s and World War II. Seventy-three percent of the victims were African American. But in the southern states, the percentage of African American victims topped 90, reflecting 3,245 black people murdered by whites within that time span.[61] Two young black men were added to that statistic during the summer that Fisher was celebrating his graduation from college and anticipating the beginning of graduate school at Union.[62] Photographs of the dead, tortured corpses of Thomas Shipp and Abram Smith, hanging from two trees and surrounded by a delighted white audience, were publicized nationwide and became the inspiration for Billie Holiday's haunting song, "Strange Fruit."[63]

On January 12, 1931, during Bonhoeffer's Sloane Fellowship year, an African American man was accused of rape in Maryville, Missouri, chained to a schoolhouse roof, and burned to death by a white mob. Bonhoeffer read the story of that lynching and viewed the graphic photographs.[64] Two months later, news of the infamous nine Scottsboro boys spread throughout the country and the world. Nine black male youths, ages thirteen to nineteen, from Scottsboro, Alabama, were rushed through trial as a mere formality by a white society nurturing an unquenchable thirst for black blood and aware that northern states were watching. The boys were condemned to death for what Bonhoeffer later described as "raping a white girl of dubious reputation." He described the boys' plight as a "terrible miscarriage of justice."[65] Bonhoeffer wrote a letter home, petitioning a German church leader to join the international protest over the Scottsboro case, but the church leader wrote back, citing a theological argument as a reason for denying his request. Over a decade later, during the church struggle in Germany, Bonhoeffer was still talking about that case as he wrote about the ethics of office and vocation.[66]

Lynching was a method of terrorism, and terror was a proven instrument wielded by the keepers of structural and systemic white

supremacy to police the borders of privilege. Whites used terrorism to condition blacks to avoid white segregated spaces and to
give way to the claims of white ascendancy in regard to all matters
related to heaven and earth. Members of societies arranged by terrorism and fear accepted their places within the artificial, socially
constructed hierarchy forced upon them by the dehumanizing narrative of race. In Jim Crow America, the narrative of race depicted
black people as subhuman, which served to legitimate brutality
against them. The narrative forced black compliance with the story
of white supremacy by training fear of violent retaliation into the
black psyche and habituating them to compliance with their artificial role as subordinates to their fully human white superiors.[67]

BONHOEFFER IN THE HARLEM RENAISSANCE

When Bonhoeffer entered Harlem with Fisher, he met a counter-
narrative to the white racist fiction of black subhumanity. The
New Negro movement radically redefined the public and private
characterization of black people.[68] A seminal moment in African
American history had arrived, and all of Bonhoeffer's descriptions
of his involvement in African American life during his Sloane
Fellowship year occurred during this critical movement. He turned
twenty-five that February. Bonhoeffer was experiencing that critical moment in African American history while he was still young
and impressionable.

The New Negro, a book containing a collection of essays, was
edited by one of the leading intellectual architects of the movement, Alain Locke.[69] The New Negro, as Locke and his authors
appropriated the term, described the embrace of a contradictory,
assertive black self-image in Harlem to deflect the negative, dehumanizing historical depictions of black people. The New Negro
made demands, not concessions: "demands for a new social
order, demands that blacks fight back against terror and violence,
demands that blacks reconsider new notions of beauty, demands
that Africa be freed from the bonds of imperialism."[70] Bonhoeffer
knew the movement by the descriptor New Negro, but James
Weldon Johnson preferred to describe the movement as the Harlem
Renaissance, rather than through the New Negro, as a rebirth of
black people rather than something completely new.[71] Johnson's
leadership role and influence in the African American community

helped to solidify his preference for Harlem Renaissance, rather than New Negro movement, as historically influential.[72]

Bonhoeffer entered Harlem and connected with new friends and ministry partners. He shared their disdain for the injustices leveled against their people, and he could empathize with their demands for dignity, as Germany hoped for a rebirth of their own dignity after the international humiliation associated with World War I. But in America, when Bonhoeffer entered Harlem, he crossed a color line that was meant to endow him with social esteem, access, and privileges that Fisher and every other person of color in the world did not have. In America, Bonhoeffer was white, and in his native Germany he would later recognize and translate his American experience of whiteness as the National Socialist references to *die Herrenvolk*, the master race.

Harlem Renaissance culture and theology were born from the experiences that African Americans had with white racist terrorism. Bonhoeffer immersed himself in Harlem and saw white America from the perspective of black "American outcasts."[73] He observed white American Christians from the "rather hidden perspective" of American outcasts in Harlem, where he witnessed a white American accommodation of religion and domination in the form of a white Christ. But with African Americans in Harlem, he did not find Christianity striving to accommodate itself to white supremacist civilized society, nor did he find the liberal Christian expression of the Berlin school of theology that trained him in Germany. In Harlem, Bonhoeffer finally heard something different. He encountered a black Christ as the subject of worship in a Christian dialogue about sin, grace, the love of God, and ultimate hope "in a form different from that to which we [Germans] are accustomed."[74]

The black encounter with Jesus was different from that which Bonhoeffer observed with the Christ of white liberals. Bonhoeffer described white modern liberal Christianity that he experienced in New York as "ethical and social idealism borne by a faith in progress that—who knows how—claims the right to call itself 'Christian.' "[75] But his experience of black Christians in Harlem recognized sin and the hope of salvation to include God's awareness of suffering and man's inhumanity to man. Christianity in Harlem also provided Bonhoeffer with a contrast to what he generally saw in white churches, where "the real point" seemed to be missing.[76] The real point of church and Christianity was apparent to Bonhoeffer in the church of the outcasts, where he heard about Jesus as the center of Christian devotion and where Jesus was celebrated "with captivating passion and vividness."[77]

BLACK JESUS

Bonhoeffer joined Fisher as a regular attendee and coparticipant at Abyssinian Baptist Church in Harlem, where Fisher was assigned to intern as a requirement of his studies at Union.[78] The language of sin and salvation was present at Abyssinian, but the white liberal modernist hope for human achievement was not. Jesus, not modernity, was the reason for hope within black Christian communities like Abyssinian. Jesus was evidence that God knows suffering; if God was with Jesus in his suffering at the hands of injustice, then surely God is with black people who suffer in America.[79] To many African American Christians, pastors in Harlem, and intellectuals of the Harlem Renaissance movement, the white Christ was a problem. He represented a type of Christianity that served only to instigate black suffering. The God represented by the white Christ could be described as sadistic; he was a transcendent pedagogue who stood at a distance, coming near only to chastise the sinner with misery.[80] In that case, the popularly pejorative images of indolent, lawless, licentious black people made suffering a natural, inevitable, even theologically appropriate part of black life. But that Christ was not worshiped in Harlem. Bonhoeffer found that black Christians identified black suffering with Jesus' suffering. Bonhoeffer heard this connection in black preaching and in black Christian music. Historically, black Christian music emphasized that Jesus' work of redemption and deliverance demonstrated his solidarity with social outcasts, even unto death.[81] That explains why the lived experience of Jesus' cross for black people in America was one of the most often repeated themes within the spirituals, as evidenced by the question in the spiritual "were you there?"

> Were you there when they crucified my Lord?
> Oh, sometimes it causes me to tremble, tremble, tremble
> Were you there when they crucified my Lord?
> Were you there when they nailed him to the tree?
> Were you there when they pierced him in the side?

Were you there when the sun refused to shine?
Were you there when they laid him in the tomb?[82]

The spirituals elevate the hope for "God with us" in a black identification with Jesus' suffering. The liberal white struggle to deter-
mine the continued relevance of Jesus was not present in Harlem.
In Harlem, African American Christians embraced the story of
Jesus, the crucified Christ, whose death they claimed paradoxi-
cally gave them life, just as God resurrected Jesus in the life of
the earliest Christian community.[83] At Abyssinian with Fisher,
Bonhoeffer found Christ existing as community where historically
marginalized and oppressed black people knew Jesus as cosufferer
and the gospel spoke authoritatively into all areas of life. Such a
Christian experience left its mark on him.[84]

BONHOEFFER, THE BLACK CHRIST
AND JEAN LASSERRE

One Sunday Myles Horton observed Bonhoeffer returning to his
seminary lodging from Abyssinian Baptist after teaching Sunday
school.[85] Bonhoeffer lingered for a time, excited to talk about
his day at church; the audience participation during the sermon
and the black spirituals were all extremely moving for him. To
Horton's surprise, Bonhoeffer was quite emotional; this was out of
character for the typically logical, unemotive Bonhoeffer. Horton
later recalled, "Perhaps that Sunday afternoon . . . I witnessed a
beginning of his identification with the oppressed which played
a role in the decision that led to his death."[86] It may be that the
spirit-filled vibrant worship of the black Christ brought home
to Bonhoeffer in a personal and emotive way the conversations
about following Jesus that he was having with Jean Lasserre and
his other friends at that time.[87] But Bonhoeffer's important relationship with Lasserre must be recognized as occurring within
his experience of entering Harlem. The transformation that was
inspired by his incarnational experience in the "church of the outcasts of America" became the lens through which the Sermon on
the Mount was seen, mobilizing it as commandments to obey from
within the context of solidarity in suffering. Suffering and obedience carried new weight for Bonhoeffer from within his "rather
hidden perspective" of solidarity with blacks who knew Jesus as
one of the oppressed.

Hence, by entering into the hermeneutic of the black Jesus in the context of oppression, Bonhoeffer's conversations with Lasserre about what Jesus expects of his followers inspired new developments in Bonhoeffer's own Christian experience. This encounter of the Harlem Renaissance Jesus and Lasserre's emphasis on the Sermon on the Mount sheds light on Bonhoeffer's abiding interest in learning from Gandhi as well. The oppressive nature of the East Indian experience yielded a similar kind of proletarian versus bourgeois experience of Christ. Lasserre represents more than another stimulating European theologian for Bonhoeffer; his emphasis on the Sermon on the Mount fit Bonhoeffer's incarnational emphasis by providing corresponding concreteness for daily Christian life in obedience to the suffering Christ whom he met while learning about theology that had developed within the African American experience under "completely different circumstances" than those he knew in Germany.[88]

ENTERING INTO JEAN LASSERRE'S CONTEXT

Lasserre also represents something that Bonhoeffer did not know in Germany. His was a very unlikely friendship for Bonhoeffer: "he was a Frenchman towards whom the loyal German in Bonhoeffer could not help feeling burning resentment."[89] Yet, Bonhoeffer moved past his initial umbrage to forge a bond with the French pastor. Bethge credits Bonhoeffer's friendship with Lasserre for the seriousness with which Bonhoeffer came to regard the Sermon on the Mount:

> In Jean Lasserre he found a man who shared his longing for the concretion of divine grace and his alertness to the danger of intellectually rejecting the proximity of that grace. His friend confronted him with the question of the relationship with God's word and those who uphold it as individuals and citizens of the contemporary world. This soon led Bonhoeffer to a new understanding of the Sermon on the Mount.[90]

With Lasserre, loyalty to Christ took another new perspective. Within the context of Bonhoeffer's traditional Lutheran ethics, the commandments of Christ did not have the same authority. His friendship with Lasserre helped bring Bonhoeffer to another level of commitment to Christ specifically regarding his newfound ecumenism and peace witness.[91]

In a letter from Tegel prison, Bonhoeffer referenced Lasserre as "the young French pastor who desired to be a saint" with whom he had had a conversation years earlier. In that letter, Bonhoeffer remembered the two of them discussing what they wanted to do with their lives. Lasserre responded that he would like to be a saint, and Bonhoeffer recalled saying that he wanted to learn to have faith.[92] One may speculate about the differences between having faith and being a saint, but what is clear is that they were both concerned to live an authentic Christian life. And in Lasserre, Bonhoeffer found another insight to help him shake loose from the deadlock of contradictory theology into a life of a Christian who "put his whole existence under the gospel," much like the theological language that Bonhoeffer recognized in the African American spirituals that he loved so much.[93] Living a faithful life requires moving beyond the language of ambitious academic conquest. It requires costly grace.

EMPATHY AND LOYALTIES

Lasserre's influence can be seen in Bonhoeffer's seminal work, *Discipleship*, in the distinction Bonhoeffer makes between what he calls "cheap grace" and "costly grace."[94] The difference between the two is the result of costly grace in a life of simple obedience to the commandments of Christ. Lasserre helped Bonhoeffer to value simple obedience to Christ's commandments as Bonhoeffer's perception of Jesus was undergoing key developments.

In the spring of 1931, Bonhoeffer and Lasserre were students at Union when they went together to see *All Quiet on the Western Front*, a movie about the Great War, World War I, made from the German perspective. German anti-French resentment was clear in the film; for example, when a German soldier shot a French soldier, the American audience cheered. American military fought alongside the French in World War I, but ironically the American audience was persuaded by the film's German viewpoint against the French. Lasserre was deeply grieved and Bonhoeffer was embarrassed.[95] But Bonhoeffer was also pained, being moved by empathy with Lasserre in the theater. Bonhoeffer witnessed his friend experiencing something like the racial acrimony that his friends in the Harlem community knew. But this time, Bonhoeffer's *Volk* sympathies shared the dominant oppressor's role with the shockingly disrespectful white American audience.

The movie experience with Lasserre evidenced a significant change in Bonhoeffer. He responded to Lasserre's grief not with "some commonplace kind of help" but with a transforming theological perspective.[96] Bonhoeffer demonstrated a new identification with a common Christian kinship in the universal body of Christ.[97] In the theater, the nationalism and deep loyalty to *Volk* that initially created contradictions in his theology suffered a significant blow. Bonhoeffer was beginning to confront the question of "the relationship between God's word and those who uphold it as individual citizens of the contemporary world [in every nation]."[98] This global development in his understanding of the way of Jesus included a new look at obedience to the Sermon on the Mount.

BONHOEFFER AND LASSERRE IN DIALOGUE

Years after Bonhoeffer's death, Lasserre published a book entitled *War and the Gospel* that articulates his argument for a Christian peace witness through obedience to Christ's concrete commands in all of life. In its pages, Lasserre describes himself as "putting objections into the mouth of an imaginary critic."[99] Lasserre's "imaginary critic" sounds much like his friend Bonhoeffer did prior to his Sloane Fellowship in New York. The conversations that Lasserre describes with his imaginary critic could easily be projected to mirror those about simple obedience to Christ that he must have had with Bonhoeffer when they met in the fall of 1930. For example, in Bonhoeffer's Barcelona lecture in 1929 entitled *Basic Questions of a Christian Ethics*, Bonhoeffer impugned the notion of a biblical Christian ethics and denied any connection between the daily life of Christians and concrete guidance from the Sermon on the Mount. He claimed that it was an "utter perversion of one's ethical sensibilities" to argue for the love of one's enemies in the time of crisis when one's *Volk* is threatened. It is especially true that in the moment of crisis, Bonhoeffer claimed, the commandments of Christ can be bracketed, taking a backseat to our more important loyalty to *Volk*. In such cases, killing could be sanctified and prove more important than slavish and unfree obedience to biblical behavioral rules.[100] In response, Lasserre spoke of Christian faithfulness in a time of crisis:

> I do not believe that the history of human society shows certain catastrophic situations where Christians could legitimately consider the Gospel's moral demands as temporarily suspended, virtually unfulfillable, during the time of the so-called crisis—so that they would thereby be released from the obligation to conform to such demands in their daily conduct. . . . The only true crisis began with the Cross, and this crisis will end only with the Lord's return; till this time Christians are called to a faithful witness. They could never be absolved from obedience to their Master by any national catastrophe or even the collapse of a civilization, nor would such things justify their being content with a cheapened version of Christianity.[101]

For Lasserre, loyalty to Christ was the only acceptable Christian response to the gospel's claims at all times. Christians must order all other loyalties by their unsurpassed loyalty to Jesus. Any other arrangement of loyalties results in a cheapened version of Christianity.

LASSERRE AND HIS INTERLOCUTOR ON COSTLY GRACE

The notion of a cheapened version of Christianity calls to mind the post–New York distinction that Bonhoeffer made in *Discipleship* between cheap grace and costly grace. Lasserre's reference to a cheap Christianity connects both men to shared arguments against Bonhoeffer's pre–New York *Volk*ish theology. In *Discipleship* there is agreement with the themes of the "faithful witness" and "obedience" that Lasserre describes above.

The pre–New York Bonhoeffer demonstrated that the guiding hermeneutic of Christ within his notion of Christ the *Stellvertretung* was still captive to German nationalism. Within the wider German public, many other Christians claimed theological justification for distorted Christian loyalties in the same manner, supporting national domination and exploitation, Hitler's notion of *Lebensraum*, under the guise of grace. Their loyalty to Christ-centered obedience was co-opted by theologically supported loyalty to Nazi ideology.

Likewise, Bonhoeffer's earlier description of God as the Lord of history sanctioning the pushing aside of other, weaker *Volk* and of Christian ethics as dependence on "human categories of good and evil" were criticisms of attempted obedience to the Bible and a distorted interpretation of God's grace.[102] Before his introduction to his friends in New York, Bonhoeffer claimed that obedience to commandments of Christ has "nothing to do with the grace of God."[103]

Similarly, Lasserre's imaginary interlocutor argues that Jesus was not a "moralist": "his aim was to go beyond the [human] categories of good and evil, to replace the letter by the spirit, obedience to the law by Communion with the Father."[104] Like Bonhoeffer in Barcelona, the critic wants to claim grace, not obedience to commandments, as the guiding substance of a Christian hermeneutic.

But Lasserre argues that obedience is what makes one Christian; believers do not move backward theologically when living in obedience to Christ: "grace can be conceived only as a dialogue between the Gospel of forgiveness in Christ, and the condemnation brought upon us by the law; if there is no more law, there is no more grace either."[105] The law to which Lasserre refers is the commandments of Christ. Knowledge of the grace of God as costly grace comes as believers live in obedience to Christ's commandments. The Christ that Lasserre describes echoes the Christ of Bonhoeffer's description of costly grace. The claim to follow Christ means concrete adherence to the commandments of Jesus in all areas of life, which included for Bonhoeffer new devotion to the Sermon on the Mount.[106]

BONHOEFFER AND COSTLY GRACE

After 1931 Bonhoeffer argued for concrete obedience to the Sermon on the Mount. As early as 1932, he wrote that, with cheap grace, Christians consider Christ's commands to be idealistic and too abstract to follow. But the grace of God calls us to discipleship; it condemns sin and justifies the sinner.[107] Costly grace opposes cheap grace, which distorts and avoids Jesus. Cheap-grace Christianity encourages bias with theological justification for the practice of oppression by the Volkish Christianity that encourages misplaced loyalties and divides the body of Christ. During the church resistance movement, Bonhoeffer railed against cheap grace—a cheapened version of Christianity—with vitriol.

Cheap grace presupposes a sinful life as the justification of sin but not the sinner.[108] Cheap grace is the preaching of forgiveness without repentance:

> It is baptism without the discipline of the community; it is the Lord's Supper without the confession of sin; it is absolution without personal confession. Cheap grace is grace without discipleship, grace without the cross, grace without the living incarnate Jesus Christ.[109]

Cheap grace describes the Christian life that Bonhoeffer formerly knew, as a Christian with divided loyalties. And during the church resistance movement against German Christian advocates of turning all Jews into outcasts and scapegoats for the problems of postwar Germany, Bonhoeffer's Christ-centered theology became radical opposition to Nazi-sympathizing cheap-grace Christianity.

Bonhoeffer remembered the plight of African Americans, and his experience of observing white Christianity from their hidden perspective became for him a shared understanding of the Jewish plight. Christianity became concrete and visible from the perspective of suffering, and, from the perspective of suffering, Bonhoeffer saw that Christians must be different from people who do not have the commandments of Christ. Bonhoeffer claimed that the obedient church is visible to the world, because Christ's claim that "you are the salt" and "you are the light" are not suggestions; they are clear commandments that Christ gives to all Christians, in whatever country they are found.

As "the light," followers of Christ are members of a visible community of faith, and their discipleship consists of evident behavior that distinguishes them from the world. Christ emphasized this when he said, "No one after lighting a lamp places it under a bushel basket, but on the lamp stand!"[110] Bonhoeffer's Harlem-inspired perspective helped him to interpret this passage for his context:

> The bushel basket, under which the visible community hides its light, can be fear of human beings [Nazis] just as much as it can be intentional conformity to the world for some arbitrary purposes, whether it be missionary purposes or whether it arises from misguided love for people [Volk]. But it may also be—and this is even more dangerous—a so-called reformation theology, which even dares to call itself theologia crucis, and whose signature is that it prefers humble

invisibility in the form of total conformity to the world over pharisaic visibility.[111]

Precisely at this junction, at the cross of Christ, Bonhoeffer's understanding of Jesus underwent significant development during his time in New York. He was put in touch with the call of obedience to the God who shares suffering with the oppressed for the sake of justice. Bonhoeffer's identification of Jesus with the marginalized and the oppressed became a perspective from which prophetic insight would make him one of the most impactful theologians of the twentieth century.

CHAPTER TWO

A THEOLOGY OF RESISTANCE IN THE HARLEM RENAISSANCE

Bonhoeffer was not excited about becoming a student again, especially in America.[1] The American academic practice of using course textbooks and a credit-earning system that imposed regulations on him by required classes with obligatory lectures and assignments was unfamiliar to him as a German scholar, and it grated against his sense of academic freedom. In Berlin Bonhoeffer charted his own way as a theology student, seeking more than what the institution or any one professor had to offer as he crafted his unique theological contribution. Becoming a student again in such an expressly regulated way was also anticlimactic for the new Ph.D. graduate, author of two dissertations, and newly appointed faculty member at the University of Berlin. Before he set foot on American soil, he was already convinced that he had nothing to learn in America about theology.[2] That is why, of all the schools in America that he could have attended, Union Seminary was attractive to him; Bonhoeffer believed that its location in New York had much more to offer than the limited potential of the American theological academy.[3]

On January 30, 1930, while he was still vacillating about the idea of studying in America, he submitted an application letter

to the German Academic Exchange Service, asking for a fellowship to study abroad. Bonhoeffer's letter said that he wanted to
gain familiarity with the American church, further his scholarly
and ecclesiological work, and to study systematic theology "as
it has developed under completely different circumstances."[4] He
briefly mentioned the subject of his first dissertation, a systematic
foundation of a sociology of the church, and described his interest in "the study of dogmatics and its relationship with its two
neighboring fields of sociology and philosophy" at an American
theological institute.[5] Bonhoeffer was not settled on his decision
to go to America until May of 1930. In May his placement at
Union was set, he received a grant from the German Academic
Exchange Service, and Union Seminary awarded him a Sloane
Fellowship. Given Bonhoeffer's thoughts about theology and the
church in Germany at this time in his life, it is no wonder that
he finally embraced the opportunity for international studies with
clarity and intent, knowing what he wanted, and did not want,
from his studies in America. But he was surprised by where his
theological interests led him. His clearly identified theological and
ecclesiological goal for study in America eventually led Bonhoeffer
into Harlem and the Harlem Renaissance.

THE HARLEM RENAISSANCE AND THE
GREAT MIGRATION

Between the late nineteenth century and the mid-1930s, Harlem,
New York, was the destination of choice for masses of people caught
on the wrong side of a global color line.[6] The Harlem Renaissance
was birthed in the course of an increasing black mobility, most
notably the Great Migration. Masses of blacks converged upon
Harlem from colonized places in the Caribbean and the southern United States. Some scholars describe the migration figuratively, as a move from the medieval to the modern.[7] Most blacks
remained in the southern states, but those who joined the migration in the early twentieth century were doing so for a number of
reasons: they were fleeing from southern farm fields and leaving
the land of perpetual white terrorism, dehumanization, and the
lynch law in pursuit of a truer democracy.[8] In their exodus toward
a new black identity, they were also seeking job opportunities

resulting from the rise in industry and World War I.[9] In the wake
of World War I, the migration became an international response
to a changed global imagination. Scholars describe the Harlem
Renaissance as an intellectual and ideological mass migration,
adding "revolutionary internationalism" to the list of factors that
contributed to the emergent New Negro figure. The New Negro
was a conceptual guide that originated after the Reconstruction,
in the desire for a fair representation of the black race to lead the
way toward a new, global, black cultural and political identity for
the twentieth century.[10]

THE HARLEM RENAISSANCE: THE ACTUALIZATION
OF A REAL PEOPLE

In *The New Negro*, Locke and his authors describe the movement as a transition from the myth of the Negro to the actualization of a real people.[11] The Great Migration coincided with this
actualization in what became the Harlem Renaissance. Both the
Great Migration and the Harlem Renaissance embodied hope that
mobilized a transition from an abstract representation by oppressive political powers of colored people as fictional characters in
a worldwide narrative of white supremacy to an authentic representation of the global "colored" world. The Harlem Renaissance
saw a proliferation of music, art, and literature that coincided with
a developing political and theological black self-understanding
in the formation of black culture from the Harlem community
in Manhattan. It was the rebirth of blackness transpiring in
America—a Renaissance in Harlem.

Bonhoeffer turned Harlem into an extension of the classroom during his academic experience in America. His study of the
African American experience corresponded with his study of the
general condition of church and theology in America, positioning him to see what W.E.B. Du Bois described as the "color line"
from the perspective of populations unfavorably situated within
it, and to reflect on his own favorable position.[12] As a creative and
impressionable young German theologian, Bonhoeffer described
his findings about the race problem in America during his year of
study, 1930–1931, as "deeply distressing."[13]

HARLEM'S INFLUENCE ON
HIS COURSE SCHEDULE

Bonhoeffer's analysis of the American church and theology in Harlem gave him insight into America's race problem from the perspective of communities subjected to white supremacy. That perspective resulted in a development within his theology between his first and second semesters at Union. He did not know Harlem when he picked his first semester classes, but during the fall semester he became a student of Harlem. He met prominent leaders of the Harlem Renaissance and studied their literature while he was enjoying the "applied Christianity" of his Harlem church community.[14] His choice of classes during the spring semester, 1931, was influenced by his fall semester experiences. Bonhoeffer's increased engagement with social ethics in the spring semester of postdoctoral work signified the transition in his theology from primarily abstract to socially concrete. In particular, his classes with Dr. Reinhold Niebuhr, Dr. Charles Webber, and Dr. Harry Ward helped him to reflect on his deeply distressing encounters in Harlem.

In the spring of 1931, he took a course that was cotaught by Professors Niebuhr and Ward entitled Ethical Viewpoints in Modern Literature.[15] In his end-of-the-year summary to the Church Federation Office, he described that course with reference to Harlem: "In a lecture course by Dr. Niebuhr, the social and Christian problem was discussed in the context of modern American literature. That was extremely informative. I learned much from my own experiences in Harlem."[16] Bonhoeffer's biographer and close friend, Eberhard Bethge, said that study with Dr. Webber exposed Bonhoeffer to "labor problems, restriction and profits, civil rights, juvenile crime, and the activity of churches in these fields."[17] The list of topics addressed in Webber's class names many of the community problems targeted by ministries that Bonhoeffer encountered at Abyssinian Baptist Church. In the same end-of-year summary to the Church Federation Office, Bonhoeffer described his spring-semester course with Webber as "the most valuable experience I had at the seminary"[18] while naming the institutions Webber's class visited: "YMCA,[19] home missions, cooperative houses, playgrounds, children's court, night school, socialist schools, homeless shelters, youth organizations, and the Association for the advancement of coloured people."[20] Bonhoeffer also took a separate course with Dr. Ward entitled Ethical Interpretations,[21] and his class notes show that he was exposed to an analysis of the southern lynch law and gender disparities within African American higher education, along with prohibition, unemployment, and hot spots of international tension.[22] Bethge argues that Bonhoeffer's desire to do ministry in Berlin's overcrowded slums upon his return home from his Sloane Fellowship was due to his exposure to Ward's spring-semester class.[23] These academic encounters in Bonhoeffer's second semester at Union were informed by his encounters in Harlem and impacted his theological outlook in such a way that he not only began to think of the concrete impact of theological claims but also later included a social focus for his theology students in 1932 at the University of Berlin.[24]

BONHOEFFER'S DISCOVERY IN HARLEM

Just as he did in Berlin, Bonhoeffer looked beyond what the institution or any one theologian had to offer him. He sought to learn all that he could in a short time and, with the help of key friendships, to make his own way in New York. His second-semester courses became tools for structured engagement with what he gained from his social encounters. After his first semester at Union, Bonhoeffer was unequivocal about his disappointment with American academic theology and ecclesiology. His scathing claim about the absence of theology in America, "there is no theology here," was written in a letter to his church superintendent, Max Diestel, on December 19, 1930, at the end of his first four months in America.[25]

In that same letter, Bonhoeffer said that in those four months he had "only heard a genuine proclamation of the gospel from a Negro."[26] The tone of the statement was astonishment; to his amazement, he was "increasingly discovering greater religious power and originality among the Negroes."[27] Yet there were at least two levels of surprise in his discovery of African American Christians. The gospel that he heard in Harlem caught his attention by its familiar theological claims of Christ-centeredness. But he found that to be Christ centered in Harlem required a different engagement with the world than that with which he was familiar. The African

American Christian community at Abyssinian that Bonhoeffer encountered was indeed Christ centered, but Bonhoeffer needed to enter the context of their encounter with Christ to recognize and to reflect on the cultural implications of how his unique theological contribution described Christ-centeredness and what Christians in Harlem meant by that term.

CUBA, THE COLONIAL WOUND, AND THE WHITE CHRIST

Ironically, Bonhoeffer's letter complaining about the appalling content of white American theology and his embrace of the "Negro" rendition of the gospel was written during Bonhoeffer's Christmas visit to Havana, Cuba, a former Spanish colonial possession struggling to gain independent stability while still nurturing what scholars describe as a "colonial wound."[28] Bonhoeffer's letter described the excellent academic status of the theological environment within the German quarter he was visiting. As he continued the letter, he revealed that his analysis of American theology did not yet reach the point of empathic identification with the Harlem Renaissance community where he had become an impromptu student. For, although he was critical of white American Christianity, Bonhoeffer's assessment of the German community in postcolonial Cuba betrayed his membership within the colonial world as an imperialist. He remained receptive to the colonialist political establishment, with its theology crafted to aid in the imperialist domination of new lands. Colonialist theology accomplished this by demanding that native inhabitants adapt and conform to it, thus taking on the worldview of the dominant power. Colonialist theology became primarily abstract and theoretical and was out of touch with the wounds that colonial domination inflicted on the indigenous peoples of color, whose suffering under colonial oppression was not abstract but concrete.

Bonhoeffer's academic goals for his time in America resulted in his learning of the connection between a racialized humanity and a racialized Christianity, with its white and black Christs.[29] The white Christ was not only present in New York but also in the colonial wound that remained in Cuba and in all other locations where imperialism lingered or left a mark. The Harlem Renaissance community in which Bonhoeffer made his church home saw itself as linked to the colonized Cuban people in a global experience of the color line and the accompanying imperialist, white-racist power structure, within which Bonhoeffer could choose to remain safe. Bonhoeffer praised the German community in Cuba and contributed to their excellent theological academic environment in the midst of the Cuban colonial wound without recognizing the existence and condition of the Cuban people still suffering from the aftereffects of colonialism and from the persistent color line. Or perhaps Bonhoeffer's remarks to Diestel are evidence that he did see something in Cuba, something that reminded him of his early impressions of Harlem. Perhaps Cuba represented the beginning of his emergence from the lingering influence of the white Christ of postcolonial German nationalism that had shaped his theology before the Harlem Renaissance.[30]

The white Christ was the theological muscle of the power structure of the color line and its global manifestations: colonization, imperialism, nationalism, and white terrorism in America. The grip of that power structure was felt differently depending upon one's location on the color line. It was constructed for white, European men like Bonhoeffer to be comfortable in its hands. But his intention to know theology developed under completely different circumstances made him vulnerable to an empathic theological experience that took Bonhoeffer into the context of oppressed people. There he learned of his own disturbing theological commitments from the perspective of others in a critical engagement with the lethal white Christ. He diagnosed a Christian problem in Harlem by access to the perspective of people who are subjected to the color line in forced compliance to white supremacy. To his credit, Bonhoeffer's empathic move included the capacity to make revisions in his theology and worldview after diagnosing a problem that was his as well.

THE WHITE CHRIST OF THE EUROPE-AS-CENTER IMPERIALISM

Bonhoeffer received his theological training within the Western European theological community that was still operating in a continuing history of imperialism and colonial domination. Germany knew an imperial history differently than did its European neighbors, and after World War I Germany's place within the imperial

European community was all the more unique as a postcolonial state in the midst of a still-colonial world.[31] The postcolonial Germany of Bonhoeffer's youth felt a collective longing for Germany's imperial past, and, as Bonhoeffer demonstrated prior to his Sloane Fellowship, Germany's festering imperialist loyalties to nation and *Volk* became synonymous with claims to Christ-centeredness for many Christians in Germany, Bonhoeffer included. To understand the implicit social assumptions that influenced and shaped the Bonhoeffer who came to experience Harlem and to understand the theological and social assumptions that were influencing the Harlem Renaissance that he was about to experience, understanding of the conflict between colonialist and postcolonialist cultural frames is necessary. Evidence shows that Bonhoeffer read many of the authors of the Harlem Renaissance; he wrote an essay assessing them.[32] Black intellectuals of the Harlem Renaissance were participants in a transnational movement that was critically examining the intersection of race and religion within modern colonialism. The Christianity birthed from that merger was crafted for a type of social resistance; it was racialized and fashioned to practice social detachment and to resist the pattern of relational intimacy and joining that would characterize the gospel's language of incarnation in order to accommodate itself to brutality and domination. The analysis of Harlem Renaissance intellectuals became a part of Bonhoeffer's Christian transformation in New York. Bonhoeffer began to learn from them theology developed under completely different circumstances, which helped to jar him loose from his spiritual and emotional deadlock.

COLONIALISM AND THE WESTERN THEOLOGICAL ACADEMY

The European theological academy that trained Bonhoeffer had historically shared a symbiotic relationship to the practice of modern colonialism, which can be summed up in two key points. First, the history of European colonialism contains the story of what Willie Jennings describes as a diseased social imagination.[33] The infection occurred when theology was merged with the colonial system to provide religious authority for centering the world on a European imagination, making Christ a white European man, and to offer an apologetics for domination and authoritarianism.

Second, the imperialist European imagination, dispersed throughout the world in the practice of colonialism and sanctified by a white Christ, also theologically justified the European invention of what W.E.B. Du Bois called the color line that belted the planet, subjugating people of color to whites-only power structures. Close analysis of this history demonstrates that the Western theological academy was not left out of this distorted relationship, but the whole Christian intellectual tradition in the West, including Germany, was impacted by the centering project of European colonialism, and the identity of the world's population was impacted by the Europe-as-center color line. The assembly of the Western theological academy began in this diseased imagination when native peoples in "discovered" lands received Christianity as a primarily evaluative practice, equipped to merge brutality and callous indifference to suffering with intellectual formation.[34] The project of theology in colonialism was split in this assembly; it was primarily doctrinal and conceptual, lacking content for Christian conduct. That split was necessary to justify the domination of foreign human bodies that accompanied classifying human beings by race, securing the advantages of whiteness, and accommodating the practices of colonialism. The lingering effect of this split was still present in Bonhoeffer's training and was evident within his Christian social sensibilities in his early inability to imagine a wholeness of life with Christ at the center, blending everyday life and religion.[35] Bonhoeffer's early sympathies for German *Lebensraum* and his corresponding Christian justification for the suffering of other *Volk* were illustrative of the lingering effects of the doctrinal versus practical split. Colonial Christianity engineered a modified theology that was bred to resist empathy and the practice of incarnation. But the practice of incarnation moves beyond an emphasis on right doctrine as the sole indicator of Christian identity to include healthy expressions of intimate joining and a faith that is social and participatory rather than primarily conceptual and abstract.

COLONIZATION AND THE EUROPE-AS-CENTER SOCIAL IMAGINATION

Until the fifteenth century, Jerusalem was the center of the Christian world.[36] From the fifteenth to the early twentieth century,

Europeans recognized their community of empires as the center of the world and the hope for humanity, culturally, geographically, and religiously.[37] In the process of colonial expansion, the Spanish "discovery" of the extreme Western continent, the *Indias Occidentales*, followed three centuries later by the invention of the Middle East and the Far East through Orientalism, Europe became the geographical, philosophical, political, economic, and spiritual center of the world.[38] What some European cartographers demonstrated on world maps was also a lived reality; the world was re-created from a perspective that established Europe as the central or fundamentally pre-eminent location on earth. The Eurocentric perspective gave to some imperialist nations the concept of "discovery," which was descriptive of a world with one history and a Christian social imagination that racialized continents as it "discovered" them, defining humanity according to the European ideal norm, as explorers came into contact with native "others" in Asia, Africa, and the Americas. Fundamentally, the Eurocentric worldview saw Europe as more than a geographical location; the language of discovery turned Europe into a people-making process.

The theological element of the Europe-as-center worldview was a Christian social imagination that was diseased by its blending with the modern European notion of ideal humanity. The diseased Christian worldview facilitated the manufacture of norms, values, and governing symbols to inform an imperialist understanding of Europeans in distinction from the natives and to provide guidance for colonial social conduct.[39] The diseased imagination was the imperialist discourse about God and humanity within the European social imagination that made colonization into a rational and spiritual good and empowered European empires to enact their reality as an objective global reality and their collective history as the only history for the planet.

GERMANY-AS-CENTER

The German Empire knew its own unique process of identity development that localized the Occidental/Oriental arrangement; Germany defined itself according to its own perceived relationship with an imagined otherness.[40] It was an imagined otherness that consisted of fellow European nations rivaling for existing colonial possessions and soon-to-be colonial possessions. German nationalism was a unique manifestation of the larger Europe-as-center mentality. In Germany, the people-making process of the Germany-as-center mentality included a eugenics-based vision of a German society ordered hierarchically by race with genuine community membership based on racial purity.[41] The difference between pre– and post–World War I German nationalist efforts toward this ideal human order was the means by which the ideal was pursued. The pre–World War I German imperialist imagination involved classifying peoples, regulating sexual interaction, and physically expanding German borders [*Lebensraum*], while post–World War I nationalism, especially under Hitler's leadership, pursued a strategy of crafting the ideal German humanity by warmongering and mass murder.[42]

THE EUROPE-AS-CENTER IMPERIALIST IMAGINATION IN THE AGE OF DISCOVERY

The language of discovery was not used by imperial Europeans to describe their introduction to a new land and people; it was descriptive of a moment of bringing geography and populations into existence by writing them into history as they corresponded with Europe—the axis of civilization. Discovery belongs to modernity, the paradigm of Europe's triumphant and imperial perspective on history, where a particular process of self-description and a local history became an objectively universal process for the advancement of civilization.[43] Modernity was an achievement of a collective European worldview and includes the story of salvation for all of humanity, and all of humanity is weighed according to its abstract definitions of ideal humanity, culture, and civilization, which were assumed to be true for the whole world. Bonhoeffer's sermon in Barcelona "Basic Questions of a Christian Ethic" disclosed a German nationalist vision of this triumphalist, imperialist modern perspective on history by reference to God as "the Lord of history" on the side of the German *Volk*.[44] Post–World War I German nationalism included the proud intermingling of German race and nation to reimagine a unified and idealized German *Volk* triumphant in their collective rebirth.[45]

COLONIAL DISCOURSE ABOUT GOD AND HUMANITY:
THE ORIGINS OF RACE

The modern European imperialist worldview introduced race as a process of classifying and assigning value within an emerging understanding that human beings exist as different types. Racialization was legitimized by a Christian endorsement of colonialism within the Europe-as-center imagination by use of a diseased theology and grossly misrepresented biblical narratives. One such narrative made use of the "curse of Ham" myth.[46] Early Spanish cartographers assigned Asia to Shem, Africa to Ham, and Europe to Japheth.[47] The "discovery" of the Americas corresponds with the European imperialist Christian cosmology in which Japheth was destined to expand, assimilate, and subjugate the identity of the inhabitants of the land into the European Christian imagination.[48] The racialization of continents corresponds with this curse-of-Ham narrative in which people of color—typically of African descent—were destined to be subjugated, and the role of Japheth was that of the blessed one to whom Ham's descendants were subjected. The impact of the Christian geopolitical worldview as described by the curse-of-Ham theory became apparent when, after the sixteenth century, it was generally accepted that the world was naturally divided into four continents.[49]

The use of the Bible in the imperial work of racializing the world was completed with the formation of the Western understanding of human beings. When modern Europeans racialized continents, they also removed the natural identifying connection that inhabitants had with their land, replacing natural, local connections with a classification scheme that employed physical features rather than geography and local traditions as a marker of human identity.[50] The racializing process worked in tandem with a European supersessionist worldview that made Europe, not Israel, the center of God's creative and salvific purpose in the world, thus burdening Europe with the task of saving and civilizing the world. The marker of membership in God's chosen European people, and of one's position in the newly emerging hierarchy of humanity, depended upon one's physical similarity to white European bodies. This was a Western scheme for human classification that was firmly established before the modern language of race was scientific. The language of race in the modern Western world was first a theological concept connected to a distorted vision of creation that reduced the understanding of non-European bodies to that of properties classified and organized by Europeans for European trade and utilization within European colonies.[51] The theology that was distorted to aid in turning bodies into commodities was mobilized by distorted claims about Jesus; Christian redemption became synonymous with assimilation into the community of God's chosen people—the European body of Christ, who saw themselves as burdened with the salvation of the world. As a result of this distortion, God's gift of salvation was now comingled with a social principle and a racial optic; social value and moral proximity to God were racialized and measured by the likeness to an idealized humanity, the white European male body. Israel was replaced by Europe as the community of God's chosen people, and Christ became a European white man.

EUROCENTRIC HUMANITY AND EMPATHY

This is the theological legacy of modern European imperialism; it brought together an unholy marriage of Christianity and imperial domination that has endured until the present with undying stamina, reproducing disfigured offspring. Human identity and social intimacy were reimagined to correspond with a racialized European Christian worldview, making Eurocentric humanity—white supremacy—the God-endorsed norm. This was not only theology tailored for colonial domination; it was also theology constructed for an identity that resisted the practice of incarnation, empathy, and transformation.[52] It took a Christianity born of the sensibilities described by incarnation, empathy, and transformation and modified it to make it resist them.[53] The Christian imperialist worldview altered Christianity in the practice of colonialism from Christ's victory over death in his body to the victory of terror and death in the subjugation of supposedly inferior populations of people. This was the theological legacy within which Bonhoeffer crafted his unique Christ-centered theology. If Bonhoeffer's Christianity was to be more than what his theological environment had to offer him, it was imperative that he see the world from a different center.

GERMANY AND THE BARBARIANS

The onset of World War I in 1914 signaled a transition in the way that the modern European community of empires viewed one another. At that time, the imperial European powers turned their cruel fantasies and their proficiently destructive weapons away from their many colonial possessions and toward one another, putting an end to the imperial era. Until 1914 the Europe-as-center model maintained a carefully constructed color line that was the product of the European hope for the progress of humanity through the triumph of modernity. But World War I unmasked the conceit that justified the color line and disproved the modern utopian claims that Europeans were the civilized leaders of humanity.[54] The war betrayed European hypocrisy by pitting one group of civilized colonizing powers against another, violently ending their fabled march toward utopia and turning the dream of human achievement into a nightmare of death and carnage. In particular, Germany's imperialist imaginations were reduced to real-world shame.

Prior to the war, the color line established the "barbarous" and the "civilized" as human categories that corresponded to the Europe-as-center, white supremacist, colonizing worldview. After the war, the label "barbaric" that Germany and other imperialists used to describe the dark-skinned colonized world became a label to describe Germany as well. In the eyes of Germany's imperialist neighbors, it became a nation of uncivilized, uncultured barbarians, now figuratively residing on the periphery of a community of civilized European nations. Since Germany was no longer considered among the world's civilized, the emerging League of Nations deemed it necessary to confiscate Germany's colonial possessions.[55] And pursuant to the restabilization of the world, the League of Nations drafted their peace treaty at their conference in Versailles, France, in June 1919.[56]

In the fall of 1930, Bonhoeffer spoke about the Versailles treaty as a painful wound "which still is open and bleeds in Germany."[57] Germany's defeat and corresponding global humiliation at Versailles stimulated a new particularly German imperial discursive process of social imagining and of identity development within the post–World War I European turn toward nation-states.[58]

THE NEW IMPERIALISM

In the newly emerging League of Nations, even governments that remained imperialist came dressed up as nation-states.[59] The turn to nation-states after World War I implied a new preference for political governance over a more limited geography managed by populations of shared culture and ethnicity, or "nationality." The idea of a League of Nations implied an international democratic process in which each nation was respected as a contributing participant in an effort for a peaceful global community. It became a sign of the international recognition of the need for healthier social imaginations by a global turn toward a democratic process of nations-in-community and away from dominating imperialist imaginations to restabilize the world.

The international transition from an imperialist global community was also felt on the underside of the color line. The turn toward democratic nation-states and away from the explicit practice of imperialism gave colonized subjects hope for freedom and, perhaps, even participation in an emergent democracy and global politics. If the end of World War I signaled the end of European imperialism and with it the belle époque of colonialism, there was a glimmer of hope among their colonial possessions that they might be granted independence. Since the highly advanced European weaponry that had been employed to force and maintain submission among the natives in the colonies had taken aim at other European powers, there was hope that the end of imperialism also meant that the weaponry would not return its focus on the colonized but that the colonized might now be included as nation-states in the efforts to realize global peace.

These hopes were not entertained by the white-centered power structures at Versailles in the League of Nations. The darker races were not permitted to participate in the conversations about world peace in the newly emerging global democracy; the colored world remained the burden of whites, who were seen as the only ones capable of responsible leadership. Although nation-states became the norm, all of Africa, and all people of African heritage that were under colonial rule, remained subject to an adoptive parent, white Western culture.[60] The global power structures continued to exist as a white world of nation-states that could not envision black Africa as part of the global body of politics:

Black colonials were not included in any imagination of world citizen-
ship occurring during the postwar discussions of peace at Versailles.
Instead, in the shift from world empires to an international League
of Nations, Europe sharpened the distinctions between empire and
republic by drawing a firm racial line between the nations and the
colonies, a color line that would then become the defining mode for
distinguishing a modern First World from an underdeveloped Third
World.[61]

The reaffirmation of their marginalization meant that a black
experience of the political transition included the conversation
not only about peace and democracy after the war but also about
black humanity. The Harlem Renaissance refigured black identity
politically, socially, and spiritually on an international scale, as
well as in the United States. Postwar events compelled many black
intellectuals to view domestic racial relations and race politics
in the United States from a global perspective. Since the League
of Nations maintained a white-supremacist worldview, people
of African descent sought a different source of identity than the
national status to which they were denied access.

Russia's Bolshevik Revolution provided an ideal of that source.[62]
The Bolshevik Revolution provided a transnational model for the
global population denied access to the newly emerging community
of nations, which proved to be a helpful social imaginary in the formation of a new black identity. The Bolsheviks modeled a connection to one another based not on national identity, as the League of
Nations did for whites, but on international proletarian solidarity.
It became a motivating force for shaping an alternative vision of
racial revolution, one in which the black diaspora became a political and spiritual transnational identification.[63] Blacks transformed
the notion of a transnational class struggle to that of a transnational race movement. Hence, the Harlem Renaissance included
its popularly known artistry and literary movement in addition
to a revolutionary black internationalism that was attracting the
underside of the color line to its specific location for the process of
reimagining identity.[64] The revolutionary black internationalism
in Harlem included blacks from within the entirety of the African
diaspora; it was a global movement that described all blacks as
connected to the colored world in their experience of the unfavorable side of the color line, which in the early 1900s included Jews
and East Indians as well as people of African descent.

BONHOEFFER IN THE HIDDEN PERSPECTIVE

When Bonhoeffer crossed the Atlantic headed to New York, he figuratively entered the space where people of African heritage were written into the story of white supremacy as modern European imperialism invented the Western world. The Atlantic Ocean played a role as an organizing symbol among Europe, America, Africa, and the Caribbean, where multitudes of black cultures were invented as African peoples were fractured into myriads of cultures and languages in the crushing weight of modern colonialism and the transatlantic slave trade.

Bonhoeffer set sail on the Atlantic Ocean and took a momentary leave of the dialogue about nation and theology within the geography of Germany's lingering imperialist imagination only to engage the conversation with Europe's white-centered ideological neighbors in America. Bonhoeffer's letter to his church superintendent, Max Diestel, from Cuba, December 19, 1930, within the vestiges of Cuba's colonial wound, takes on further meaning in the Atlantic, highlighting the influence of that different ideological space on his German-centered theological legacy. His disdain for the white representation of Christ and Christianity and the more attractive conversation about Christ that he encountered among the "Negroes" reveals Bonhoeffer's movement toward a different theological center and underscores the impact for him of that transitional discursive space and moment that was occurring on the underside of the color line.

CHAPTER THREE

BONHOEFFER IN THE VEILED CORNER
Jesus in the Harlem Renaissance

Within a stream of global change and black revolutionary internationalism, Harlem during this period was a theo-political space
for an emerging global discourse on race, religion, and politics. At
the heart of race terror in America, and in the European colonies,
was a modern notion that Europeans represented ideal humanity
and the center of civilization, while the natives and indigenous
inhabitants in the colonies represented the periphery of civilization
and inferior humanity. The notion of inferior humanity was fueled
by a distorted theological identity that made European civilization
and Christianity synonymous with one another. W.E.B. Du Bois
described this distorted theological identity in 1903:

> The characteristic of our age is the contact of European Civilization
> with the world's underdeveloped peoples. . . . War, murder, slavery,
> extermination, and debauchery—this has again and again been the
> result of carrying civilization and the blessed gospel to the isles of the
> sea and the heathen without the law.[1]

Du Bois, Alain Locke, and a large number of African American
women and men were joined by a host of Caribbeans of African
descent as intellectuals of the Harlem Renaissance and architects
of another concept of black humanity, one that did not speak from

the European "center of civilization" worldview but from the margins. From their location in modern racial discourse, Harlem Renaissance intellectuals shaped a literary movement that spoke about black culture, black political agency, and a black Jesus.[2] Their descriptions of a black Jesus were theologically disruptive to white supremacy and at times graphic, in their explicit rebukes of the oppressive and violent white Christ. Theology from the margins was, for its constituents, antivenom to the toxic theological imagination of racist colonial Christianity. The white Christ of the modern colonial construct was complicit in race terror as an opiate Jesus who sedated black people, convincing them to accept racism and subhumanity as divinely ordained by God. But the intellectual architects of blackness in Harlem portrayed Jesus in a way that decentered Europe and whiteness as the source of all saving knowledge. The forced worldview of the one-history white supremacy combined with the history and perspective of the marginalized generated border thinking. This was the epistemological process of the groups of people whose cooperation with the modern imperialist center of civilization scheme was realized only by force.[3]

Harlem was home to a gathering population of humanity on the periphery of the European construct of culture and civilization, and the practice of border thinking gave to Harlem Renaissance intellectuals a perspective of whiteness that was not available to whites, who were beneficiaries of the worldview arranged by modern imperialism. Their perspective on the imperialist worldview from the borders was like that of a fish in a stream that is capable of seeing the stream from the shore; it was a view of the dominant discourse on race and humanity by people of color subjected to the narrative of civilization as assimilated inferiors and prohibited from participation in it as contributing members. Marginalized populations experienced the imperialist worldview from the inside by force as subjects of the narrative of ideal humanity and from the outside as perpetual aliens in a whites-only world.

DU BOIS AND THE TREATY OF VERSAILLES

W.E.B. Du Bois was one of the pre-eminent African American minds of the twentieth century and a leading architect of the Harlem Renaissance's development of a new global black image within the hidden perspective of the border.[4] In 1919 Du Bois attended the Versailles Peace Conference, along with twenty-five other representatives of the NAACP, the new organization that he helped to construct. Du Bois and his entourage had hopes of talking with President Woodrow Wilson at the conference about the future of Africa, but they were unable to do so. The Versailles conference maintained a paternalistic attitude toward colonized people, and President Wilson did not grant Du Bois and his entourage, nor any other representatives of colonized peoples, an audience. Du Bois' group left Versailles disappointed.[5] Indeed, the outcome of the 1919 Versailles Peace Conference was not only disappointing for Germany, which was depicted as the world's enemy of peace; the Versailles Peace Conference was disappointing for people of color, who remained in a position of forced compliance to whatever terms for peace and participation in a global democracy were handed to them.

THE VEILED CORNER AS A CRITICAL VANTAGE POINT

One year later, in 1920, Du Bois published *Darkwater: Voices from within the Veil*, as a sequel to his groundbreaking *Souls of Black Folk*, published in 1903. Du Bois began *Darkwater* with a postscript instead of an introduction, where he uses a theological trope of Christian identity to locate his vantage point within a white-supremacist society. He writes, "I have been in the world, but not of it."[6] Du Bois is referencing Jesus' words in John 15:19 to his disciples that they are "not of the world." Some Christians understood Jesus to mean that his followers should disengage from the broader society, but Du Bois makes use of Jesus' words to give theological basis for his observation of white society and politics:[7]

> I have seen the human drama from a veiled corner, where all the outer tragedy and comedy have reproduced themselves in microcosm from within. From this inner torment of souls, the human scene without has interpreted itself to me in unusual and even illuminating ways.[8]

The veiled corner is hidden to the white majority. It gives the black observer residing on the border a truer representation of the dominant streams of consciousness on both sides of the color line than that which is offered by the one-history-fits-all, white-centered worldview. The veiled corner is the vantage point that Bonhoeffer references when he describes the African American community as "a rather hidden perspective."[9] From the hidden perspective it is apparent that racism prohibits authentic Christian discipleship.

Du Bois' notion of the veil describes a mechanism of racialization. The veil operates like a projector screen for the forced attribution of racial identity by white people upon black bodies. Du Bois argues that real black selves are hidden "within" or behind "the veil."[10] That is also the reason for what Du Bois describes as double consciousness in *Souls*; blacks hold in tension the knowledge of how whites see them within the veil and the self-knowledge of who they know themselves to be behind the veil. In *Souls* Du Bois describes "double consciousness" and "the veil" as hermeneutical keys to the interpretation of the black/white encounter. But Du Bois did not encourage black voyeurism from behind the veil; Du Bois was an advocate of resistance inspired by theological convictions.[11]

"CREDO"

Du Bois names his convictions in a statement of faith following his postscript that he entitled "Credo." In his faith statement, he drew upon the format and style of the Apostles' Creed with a set of affirmations that begin with "I believe." He describes God as the Creator of all of humanity, linking contemporary racism with concerns faced by the first-century church by referencing Acts 17:26: "I Believe in God who made of one blood all nations that on earth do dwell. I believe that all men, black, brown and white, are brothers."[12] In the history of American slavery, Acts 17:26 was a key component of the Christian abolitionist tradition of biblical interpretation. Du Bois' reference to it was an engagement with a Christian resistance to white supremacy.[13] Du Bois' description of God the Creator of all shares the inclusive ecumenical worldview of the global Christian that became important for Bonhoeffer after his time in New York. Accordingly, racial and national loyalties are oppositional to an authentic Christian witness, and Bonhoeffer became aware of that contradiction in New York.

Du Bois makes contextual references to his post–World War I audience by addressing Jesus as the Prince of Peace and drawing upon the Beatitudes to claim that the meek and lowly African Americans trapped on the underside of whites-only power would "yet inherit this turbulent earth."[14] Du Bois' christological themes are concretely this-worldly and comprise sharp criticisms of the dominant streams of abstract theological discourse within power structures to imagine Jesus suffering among today's marginalized and outcast people. By doing so, Du Bois highlights a christological problem with the white-centered global power structures; in their racism, white theological and cultural leaders crafted a counterfeit Christ whose sole job was to legitimize their racialized social imagination. White power structures created a racist Jesus. The man-made white Jesus disallowed them from recognizing the real Christ, whom they wanted to avoid, as Blum describes:

> Du Bois suggested that southern whites' racial phobias and their ignorance of human diversity led them not only to confuse African Americans with Middle Easterners, but also to overlook the Son of God. Du Bois believed that white Americans would consider a messiah of Middle Eastern descent as unthinkable as one of black heritage.[15]

Racism turns white Christians into idol worshippers, and disallows authentic Christian discipleship. For Du Bois, Jesus was consistently associated with the oppressed and was a representative of liberation and justice. To disclose this Jesus, Du Bois favored biblical references to a global family in Christ and Jesus' emphasis on peace in the Sermon on the Mount:

> There comes a priest of the meek and lowly
> Jesus—a Servant of the Servant who said
> Blessed are the Meek,
> Blessed are the Poor,
> Blessed are the Merciful,
> Blessed are the Peace-makers,
> Blessed are the Persecuted.[16]

Du Bois' use of Jesus' Sermon on the Mount was a rebuke of dominant political authorities who saw no incongruity between domination of the poor, white supremacy, and Christianity. Du Bois' evaluation of white Christianity was appealing to Bonhoeffer, as his time in Harlem was helping him to see a different interpretation of Christ-centeredness and to reflect more on the social impact of faith in Christ. For Du Bois, the Sermon on the Mount was evidence that the practice of real Christianity could deflect the vicious, dominating nature of the color line. He depicts Jesus in opposition to the modern world's power systems that were designed to favor whites only. His narratives of Jesus describe the white keepers of the color line as wealthy, proud, and belligerent people who claimed to follow Jesus while steadfastly rejecting him.[17]

"JESUS CHRIST IN TEXAS"

Du Bois placed a narrative of Jesus in the center of his essays in *Darkwater*.[18] The intent was obvious; Du Bois' essays were centered on a liberating Jesus of color. The parable "Jesus Christ in Texas" entertains a question of American Christology based on Jesus' historical background: How would the Jewish messiah be received if he were in the racist American south today? In a white-supremacist America that embraces popular claims to be a Christian nation, Du Bois depicts Jesus as a "stranger" and a constant disruption to entrenched systems of oppression. Du Bois' Jesus encounters three different scenarios with whites and blacks in Waco, Texas: outside of a prison, in the home of a wealthy white Christian couple, and in a rural country farm scene where a lynching occurs.

The parable begins with an encounter between prison officials and the stranger. The arrangement between prisoner and prison system is depicted as a miniature of European imperialism and its colonial order. White supremacy has created relationships with others according to its racialized people-organizing social imagination. But the racial organizing system is, at its base, driven by insidious loyalties to capitalism. Black bodies become fungible commodities in a white-supremacist society that nurtures deep, insidious loyalties to capitalism. Du Bois illustrates these loyalties with a conversation between a prison guard and a colonel about a black prisoner. The guard opines, "That nigger there is bad, a born thief, and ought to be sent up for life; got ten years last time." The black prisoner's subjugation to the powers of the racist legal system is justified by the prisoner's racially codified predisposition to immorality, which is an arrangement that calls to mind the supersessionist theo-political sensibilities of whiteness within colonialism; in a white-centered world, morality and racial identity are comingled and measured in proportion to the physical likeness to white bodies. But the conversation soon betrays the capitalist motives operating within the prison officials' opinion of the black reprobate: the black prison population is fodder for a lucrative business venture.

> "The convicts" he said, "would cost us $96 a year and board. Well we can squeeze this so that it won't be over $125 apiece. Now if these fellows are driven, they can build this line within twelve months. It will be running by next April. Freights will fall fifty per cent. Why man, you'll be a millionaire in less than ten years. . . ." The colonel started . . . the word millionaire sounded well to his ears.[19]

The prison system in Du Bois' narrative is a capitalist ruse of modern white supremacy. It is a remanufactured slavocracy carrying out the entrepreneurial schemes of white American imperialists. Jesus is suddenly present and interrupts the conversation between the prison guard and the colonel with a targeted question aimed at their unspoken loyalties. Jesus, the tall stranger, asks: "It will be a good thing for them?"[20] Put differently, the question becomes, "Is that loving your neighbor?" The question disturbs the colonel, and he asks, "What is this man doing here anyway?"[21] Even in the dark, the stranger's gaze is as disturbing as his words, and the colonel is compelled to vindicate himself by inviting the stranger to be his guest to a dinner party at his house. There, in the colonel's home, another significant disruption occurs.

The colonel's wife assumes the stranger to be an educated European, perhaps a teacher.[22] Hence, she is thrilled to include him among their dinner party guests as a new member of their community. From the perspective of the colonel and his wife, this initial interaction with the stranger is meant as an honor by including him among their privileged social group as one of their own. The colonel is an elite man of stature and breeding, and he enjoys high esteem within a circle of his racial and social peers.[23] But the honor extended to the stranger in the colonel's house turns quickly to outrage when they finally see the stranger's physical appearance. He is not their racial and social peer. He is not white:

> Why, the man was a mulatto, surely, even if he did not own the Negro blood, their practiced eyes knew it. He was tall and straight and the coat looked like a Jewish gabardine. His hair hung in long close curls far down the sides of his face and his face was olive, even yellow.[24]

Why would the stranger's appearance cause the colonel and his wife to turn so quickly from interest and inclusion to despising and rejecting him? Their Christian imagination is infected with white supremacy, which causes them to recoil in Jesus' presence. Their social imagination depends on their "practiced eyes" for policing the boundaries of the color line, but they cannot label Jesus' racial appearance. Du Bois hints at the stranger's race in the description of his coat, curls, and olive skin. But it was common for whites in Du Bois' narratives to confuse Middle Easterners for Negroes. To the colonel and his wife, he could be Jewish, a mulatto, or a Negro; they cannot tell. Whatever he is, he is not white. Du Bois' narrative did not claim Jesus exclusively for blacks; he imagined the historical Jesus to identify with the entire community of the unwelcomed and oppressed on the wrong side of the color line. The unwelcomed guest brought blackness, Jewishness, and a host of potential other colored people into the colonel's whites-only space, defying the skilled, racially cognizant gaze of his elite hosts and exposing their true loyalties. In the end, racist Christians actually rebuff what they claim to be their exclusive possession; they divinize whiteness, demonize color, and reject Jesus. This moment in Du Bois' parable represents the tragic irony of the color line in a Christian society; in a white-centered world, Jesus becomes a frightening disruption, another sin to be eliminated when whites disregard Jesus' embodied history as a member of the population on the unfavorable side of the color line. Two years after his time in New York, during the church struggle in Germany, Bonhoeffer would insist that exclusion of the Jews from Christian churches should also indicate the exclusion of everyone who identifies with Jesus.[25]

White uneasiness with people of color fades, however, when "colored folks" accept a compliant role within the structures of white domination. The colonel's home represents the *Pax Romana* for people of color and the ideal white supremacist, patriarchal society of the modern power structures. In a particularly poignant moment, Jesus encounters a rector among the colonel's dinner guests. The rector is a representative of the means by which the Western Christian imagination became diseased; he personifies the intermingling of Christian theology with structures of white supremacy as a welcome guest in the racist modern structure that is the home of the colonel and his wife. Jesus passes by the rector and says to him, "I never knew you," as he departs the colonel's house, into the night.[26]

Jesus' final encounter in Waco traces the racial ideology of the white theo-political world to its customarily deadly conclusion. On a road, Jesus meets an escaped black convict fleeing from bloodhounds.[27] The convict, a victim of white racist domination, confesses his crimes to Jesus, and with his confession prophecy is fulfilled: "the convict looked down at his striped clothes, but the stranger had taken off his long coat; he had put it around him and the stripes disappeared!"[28] The empathic encounter with the escaped convict begins the explicitly historical identification of Jesus and African Americans. Immediately after his nighttime encounter with Jesus, the now-freed convict quickly becomes subject to a cruel white farmer who treats him like a slave. But it is the farmer's wife who unleashes the full cruelty of white supremacy upon the freed convict after she is appalled by her personal encounter with the stranger, Jesus. In a moment of anger and panic, the farmer's wife flees from him when his social demands to extend love of neighbor to blacks reveal that the stranger is not white. In her haste to run from Jesus, she collides with the convict, who was running to Jesus. This ironic collision, white flight from Jesus and his too-demanding social expectations and black pursuit of Jesus' inclusive, humanizing social expectations, leads to the climactic moment in this narrative of Jesus from the "veiled corner." The freed convict becomes another lynched victim of white supremacy on the strength of the old and tired accusation of a black male assault on a white woman. The farmer's wife finally recognizes the stranger as Jesus when she observes the innocent black man swaying in a noose from a tree. The farmer's wife sees the stranger with him, above and behind him on a cross, superimposing himself on the dying man's image:

> She knew. Her dry lips moved: "Despised and rejected of men." She knew, and the very horror of it lifted her dull and shrinking eyelids. There heaven-tall, earth-wide, hung the stranger on the crimson cross, riven and blood-stained, with thorn-crowned head and pierced hands. She stretched her arms and shrieked.[29]

But the stranger on the cross was focused in his concerned gaze on the writhing, dying body of the thief in the noose, and the narrative

ends with Jesus' words, "this day, thou shalt be with me in para-
dise."[30] The noose becomes a symbol of saving grace, replacing it
as the commonly known symbol of white racist terrorism by representing Christ's cosuffering, empathic pursuit of justice. Seeing
the noose in this light reinterprets the location of God's revelation
in Christ; Jesus is not found among the participants of domination
and authoritarianism, nor does Jesus approve of the Christianity
that has historically endorsed systemic and structural oppression. Jesus is found among the victims of systemic and structural
oppression, repeatedly rejected, and finally killed by its guardians,
because of his empathic identification with all victims of injustice. Du Bois' narrative suggests that to die at the hands of white-
supremacist Christians is tantamount to Christian martyrdom.

CLAUDE McKAY'S "THE LYNCHING"

The theme of Christ's presence with the oppressed was common
in Du Bois' "lynching parables."[31] Du Bois argued that the historical Jesus would be unwelcomed in a Christian society that is at
home with white supremacy. In their general religious devotion,
white-supremacist Christians are participants in Jesus' crucifixion because, in truth, their Christianity was not about Christ;
white racists wedded Jesus to white supremacy, shaping Christian
discipleship to govern a racial hierarchy. Thus, rather than reject
Jesus, Du Bois represents a Harlem Renaissance stream of African
American academic and religious thought that reclaimed Jesus by
imagining his historical connection to persecuted minorities as one
who was also subjected to an abusive empire.[32] In America, Jesus'
historical connection to persecuted minorities resulted in seeing
him as black and viewing innocent black victims of white terrorism in light of Jesus' passion.[33] Blackening Jesus helped African
Americans to reimagine him outside of the structures of white-
supremacist religion.

Other Harlem Renaissance authors followed Du Bois' lead
with lynching parables that blackened Christ's body. In 1922
Jamaican poet Claude McKay's "The Lynching" connected Jesus
with the persecution of the black community by depicting Jesus as
a wronged child of God whom God was calling back to Heaven:

His spirit is smoke, ascended to the high heaven.
His father, by the cruelest way of pain,
Had bidden him to his bosom once again.
The awful sin remained still unforgiven.
All night a bright and solitary star
(Perchance the one that ever guided him,
Yet gave him up at last to Fate's wild whim)
Hung pitifully o'er the swinging char.
Day dawned, and soon the mixed crowds came to view
The ghastly body swaying in the sun.
The women thronged to look, but never a one
Showed sorrow in her eyes of steely blue;
And little lads, lynchers that were to be,
Danced round the dreadful thing in fiendish glee.[34]

McKay's poem paints a gruesome picture of the aftermath of a lynching. The detail of McKay's depiction draws parallels between Jesus' crucifixion while also recovering the horror of lynching as a ghastly public act that was robbed of its shock and turned into pornography of black suffering. An appropriate human response to the lynched, smoldering, dead black body hanging in public view does not come from the white onlookers. Children should be terrified, and the spectacle should generate some compassion for the obvious cruelty it illustrates. But the lynchers are unrepentant, and thus unforgiven, as they dance in celebratory glee at the sight of their grisly deed. McKay's poem invokes the practice that some whites engaged in of sharing pictures of dead lynched black bodies, in a celebratory fashion, as mementos of family events. Bonhoeffer viewed photographs of at least one such lynching during his Sloane Fellowship. By connecting the passion of Christ with the tortured and lynched black body, McKay and other Harlem Renaissance writers exposed the illicit nature of white lust for black blood.

GEORGIA DOUGLAS JOHNSON'S "CHRISTMAS GREETINGS"

In 1923 Georgia Douglas Johnson's "Christmas Greetings" described faith in Christ as dissonant within the African American experience. The poem illustrates the uneasy connection of hope, struggle, and generosity in a black reception of Christ:

Come brothers, lift on high your voice,
The Christ is born, let us rejoice!

And for all mankind let us pray,
Forgetting wrongs upon this day.
He was despised, and so are we,
Like Him we go to Calvary;
He leads us by his bleeding hand,
Through ways we do not understand.
Come brothers, lift on high your voice,
The Christ is born, let us rejoice!
Shall we not to the whole world say—
God bless you! It is Christmas Day![35]

Johnson's poem speaks of the coming of Christ and a connection to Christ, not in power, or in a full, final account of understanding of God and God's will. The connection with Christ that Johnson describes occurs in the suffering of Christ, and of black people. Connecting with Christ in this way allows for full honesty about the absurdity of suffering, the limits of human understanding, and the hiddenness of God.[36]

LANGSTON HUGHES' "CHRIST IN ALABAMA"

Langston Hughes' highly controversial poem "Christ in Alabama" is meant to shock readers beginning with the very first lines, "Christ is a Nigger / Beaten and black." Hughes' poem immediately identifies Jesus with African Americans who comprise a population of extant aliens among white Christians in the south; blacks are present but they do not belong. As a southern alien, Hughes' Christ is also a despised mongrel, an unholy hypostatic union of black and white races who is the bastard son of a raped black female slave and her lustful master, a white imperial God-man:[37]

Mary is His Mother:
Mammy of the South,
Silence your mouth.

God is His father:
White Master above
Grant Him your love.

Most Holy bastard
Of the bleeding mouth
   Nigger Christ
   On the cross
   Of the South.[38]

The theological and social implications of Hughes' Christ were tremendous. Hughes' view from the veiled corner highlights a white imperial God-Man who functions as a creator ex nihilo, possessing and violently inseminating the earth, subjecting the world to his will, and trumpeting himself as a savior from sin. That is a natural conclusion to European imperialists taking Christ out of his Jewish cultural history and making of him a trope of their cultural longing: a white-centered world became the community of God's chosen people and the image of their ideal cultural and national selves. Christ became a divine ideal of white imperialists to establish their God-given duty to dominate pagans. By blackening Christ, Hughes' poem, like Du Bois' Jesus narrative, highlights the racist, patriarchal imagination operating within the dehumanizing social powers of a white-centered worldview.

Writers like Du Bois, McKay, Johnson, and Hughes were prolific within the literary movement that shaped the Harlem culture of Bonhoeffer's experience. At Abyssinian Baptist Church, members were aware of these authors and their writings by their circulation in popular African American magazines like the NAACP's *Crisis*, and the National Urban League's *Opportunity*. Bonhoeffer encountered these works through his own extensive extracurricular research in addition to the exposure he gained while studying with Niebuhr. Bethge indicates that Bonhoeffer collected publications of the NAACP and read a great deal of African American literature published in other venues, likely including these magazines.[39] Both magazines were major clearinghouses for Harlem's literary movement, and by paying attention to them Bonhoeffer was exposed to the notable currents within the Harlem Renaissance. He knew of the literary movement's depictions of Jesus, which were also present in the Christianity at Abyssinian and were active in his turn from German nationalism and into incarnational "joining in" with the struggles of Jews in Germany. An obvious piece of evidence of Bonhoeffer's familiarity with these portrayals of Jesus was Bonhoeffer's reference to Countee Cullen's popular poem "The Black Christ."

COUNTEE CULLEN'S "THE BLACK CHRIST"

Written in 1929, Cullen's poem does the same work of highlighting by blackening that other Harlem Renaissance artists and intellectuals were doing. Of the numerous works by Harlem Renaissance writers that Bonhoeffer read and wrote about, this poem by Cullen is the only one Bonhoeffer directly referenced by name.[40]

Cullen's "The Black Christ" is like Du Bois' lynching parables, imagining Christ identifying with the contemporary marginalized victims of white supremacy. With Cullen, the historical Jesus is described as the first in a succession of lynched black men in the south:

> How Calvary in Palestine,
> Extending down to me and mine,
> Was but the first leaf in a line,
> Of trees on which a Man should swing
> World without end, in suffering.[41]

But Cullen articulates some of the disdain within the Harlem Renaissance for Christianity, which was viewed by some as no more than a reflex of white domination. Bonhoeffer picked up on that disdain in his report home after his first semester at Union, when he claimed that "among the youth, who see how Christian preaching made their fathers so meek in the face of their incomparably harsh fate, an element of opposition against such forms of religion is emerging, that is, against Christianity."[42] The "form of religion" that Bonhoeffer saw being opposed in the Harlem Renaissance consisted of Jesus as a Christian endorsement of white supremacy and a sedative for the cruelty of its racist Christian society. It was a Jesus who was central to the worldview responsible for the creation and maintenance of the color line. Cullen was one of the more notable young Harlem Renaissance poets when "The Black Christ" was written, and one articulating black disdain for this problem. He wrote "The Black Christ" as a voice from the black periphery while traveling in France. He began the poem by naming the audience to whom the poem was directed, "hopefully dedicated to white America," as he poetically described the tension around suffering within African American Christianity.[43]

The poem is set in the racist south, and it uses three characters to tell its story: a Job-like, pious, Christian, black mother and her two young adult sons, of whom the elder functions in a role that resembles the biblical Job's accusatory friends. Both of these young men, a younger one named Jim, in addition to the older unnamed brother, wrestle with questions of theodicy; since his childhood, Jim has doubted the existence of God because of white cruelty and innocent suffering:

> "A man was lynched last night."
> "Why?" Jim would ask, his eyes star-bright.
> "A white man struck him; he showed fight.
> Maybe God thinks such things are right."
> "Maybe God never thinks at all—
> Of us," and Jim would clench his small,
> Hard fingers tight into a ball.
> "Likely there ain't no God at all . . .
> God could not be if he deemed right,
> The grief that ever met our sight."[44]

Jim's tone is problematic for his older brother, the narrator. The older brother fears for Jim, who is voicing doubts about Christianity that the older brother has not dared to speak. But even worse, Jim's criticism of God also challenges the southern social structure. The older brother's fears and doubts are intermingled with his love for Jim, a proud and handsome young black man. White women are attracted to him, which spells certain doom. The combination of Jim's confidence and attractiveness lead his older brother to conclude that Jim must leave the south. The elder brother describes the south as a place where white domination is administered by Christians and physically enforced by terrorism. The south is cursed; it is a place of rampant inhumanity. These problems in the south fuel the elder brother's unspoken doubts about the religion of his mother:

> "Nay, I have done with deities
> Who keep me ever on my knees,
> My mouth forever in a tune
> Of praise, yet never grant the boon
> Of what I pray for night and day.
> God is a toy; put him away."[45]

The older brother's theological questions are given voice by Jim's boldness. An untold number of contradictions exist for blacks in a white racist Christian world that he will now dare to entertain: Does God have anything to give the poor, abused sufferers on earth? Or are those afflicted by oppression supposed to wait through their harsh suffering for peace in death? If God can provide safety and material needs in life but does nothing, what good is God? Is God a white racist? The narrator does not mince words about his perspective on the Christian God. Indeed, it is best to put God away or

> Make you one of wood or stone
> That you can call your very own,
> A thing to feel and touch and stroke,
> Who does not break you with a yoke . . .
> Nor promise you fine things aloft
> While back and belly here go bare,
> While his own image walks so spare
> And finds this life too hard to live
> You doubt that He has ought to give.[46]

The elder brother's disdain runs deep in his suggestion that black people fashion their own Christian idol. The disdain is related to theodicy: God's loving goodness and sovereign powers are attributes that cannot be held together in the experience of cruelty. He cannot be both all-powerful and good. The world, as the recipients of white terror experience it, does not see the good, loving, almighty Christian God. The narrator concludes that God is almighty but ambivalent, and thus God is not good. This conclusion corresponds better with their experience of the God of the white power structures.

Yet to conclude that God is simply ambivalent still does not speak to the problems with racist Christianity that Cullen identifies. Why should the ambivalent God also inspire hatred and violence against blacks? This is further reason for blacks to reject all talk of the Christian God and make another deity:

> Better an idol shaped of clay
> Near you, than one so far away.
> Although it may not heed your labors,
> At least it will not mind your neighbors.[47]

The elder brother has posed this set of questions and suggestions to his mother, who approaches her faith as Job did, not wavering in her conviction that God remains faithful despite their obvious trials. Faith is not as her sons describe; it is neither a naïve acceptance of an ambivalent deity nor a submissive acceptance of their harsh fate in a white society. Faith in God is trust in the infinite wisdom of the Creator above our own. It is also teleological, giving hope for a way of living today that is powerful enough to withstand the evils of society. Faith in God is trust that becomes

Our magic wand. Through it
We and eternity are lit.
The slave can meet the monarch's gaze
With equal pride, dreaming to days
When slave and monarch both shall be,
Transmuted everlastingly,
A single reed blown on to sing
The glory of the only King.[48]

Faith becomes the source of dignity for the oppressed, as the belief in a God who levels unjust social hierarchies. Hence, God is not white; God is the architect of a truer community, one in which all are equals, one that their mother sees by faith.

The argument between the mother and the elder son is representative of black anguish and of both sides of the disputes about Christianity in the Harlem Renaissance. The elder brother in Cullen's poem represents the discomfort with Christianity for some younger generation of African Americans whose life experiences were primarily in the north and mostly absent of the terror that life in the southern states inflicted upon their parents and grandparents. The younger Harlem Renaissance generation of African Americans perceived Christianity as a white racist religion and an opiate that served their elders as mollified prey to rabid white racists. Cullen explores the dimensions of this argument over Christianity and black anguish by making the younger of the two brothers face a lynch mob, at his home, before his mother and elder brother. The lynching scene unfolds like gospel accounts of Jesus in the garden of Gethsemane,[49] "I am he whom you seek,"[50] and before Pilate:[51]

"Lynch him! Lynch him!" O savage cry,
Why should you echo, "Crucify!"[52]

And while Jim swings from a tree, dying in a noose, the elder brother and the mother are significantly divided in their grief. The mother finds solace in her faith in God, and her eldest son despises her for it:

Above the howling winds of doubt,
How she knew Whom she traveled to

> Was judge of all that men might do
> To such as she who trusted Him
> Faith was a tower for her, grim
> And insurmountable . . .
> Anger smote me and most despair
> Seeing her still bow down in prayer.

Her continued dependence on God in the face of white terrorism merely exaggerates the elder brother's grief. His reaction to his mother's prayers in the face of their suffering resembles that of Job's wife: "Do you still hold fast your integrity? Curse God and die!"[53] But God is not the primary target of the elder brother's derision. The elder brother is mocking the Christian justification for white terrorism and black subjugation; he is rebuking his mother's white Christ:

> "Call on him now," I mocked, "and try
> Your faith against His deed, while I
> With intent equally as sane,
> Searching a motive for this pain,
> Will hold a little stone on high
> And seek of it a reason why.
> Which, stone or God, will first reply . . . ?
> What has He done for you who spent
> A bleeding life for His content?
> Or is white Christ, too, distraught
> By these dark skins His Father wrought?[54]

Cullen makes a connection among all people on the earth, like that of Du Bois' "Credo," based on the Fatherhood of God who "wrought" all the peoples of the earth. As white racist Christians indiscriminately subjugate and terrorize blacks in the south, their white Christ becomes motivation for behavior like that of Cain, who in pride and anger killed his innocent, righteous brother Abel. Yet Abel's voice could not be silenced even after he was killed.[55] Both Cain and Abel worshipped God, and similarly there is Christianity on both sides of Jim's lynching, from white killers and black victims. But God did not endorse Cain's worship or his brutality toward his brother, and neither is God on both sides of the lynching.

The white Christ is a product of the modern human classification scheme of racialization that fetishizes white European males as ideal humanity. The white Christ is the divine representative of white supremacy and a constant threat to the well-being of Jim's black family. The white Christ can only hurt, humiliate, and kill them. But the heart of Cullen's critique of Christian white supremacy discloses a different Christ-centered reality; the religion of the pious, black Christian mother has nothing to do with the religious representation of white supremacy. She is not praying to a white Christ. The Christ she worships betrays the lethal nature—for victims and perpetrators alike—of the mixture of race terror and Christianity that white racist Christians force society to drink. Her faith in Christ extracts him from that lethal concoction and disassociates him from the structures that fail to acknowledge his life in solidarity with the oppressed. Her Jesus is very different from the Christ who is co-opted by forces that turn him into a weapon wielded against marginalized people in a world built on a Manichaean interpretation of humanity. With her, Jesus becomes a contradiction to the way in which white racist Christians construct society. Her Jesus cannot be found in the domination and race-based privileges of racialized communities. She knows that Christ is hidden from racists in and among their victims, with those whom Bonhoeffer in a sermon shortly after returning from his Sloane Fellowship would later describe as the poor and the outcast who are consoled by God.[56] Indeed, Christ was hidden even from her own son, who did not know that Jesus was there, among them, until he came to recognize him in his brother's suffering.

Jim is the embodiment of God's justification of his mother's devotion to the empathic, suffering Christ. God distinguishes her faith over that of Jim's murderers and validates her faith by causing Jim to rise again from the dead:

> "Bear witness now unto His grace";
> I heard my mother's mounting word,
> "Behold the glory of the Lord,
> His unimpeachable high seal . . ."
> For there he stood in utmost view
> Whose death I had been witness to;
> But now he breathed; he lived; he walked;
> His tongue could speak my name, he talked.[57]

Jim's resurrection helps the doubting brother see Christ's love for their family and Christ's empathic joining with them in their plight, which in turn draws Jim's family into the full awareness of Christ's suffering at Calvary and the power of Christ's resurrection. Now the elder brother's crisis of faith has a resolution: he sees that the white-centered world that parades as Christian is in fact better described as a community of Christ's enemies, whose rebellion against God leads to innumerable crucifixions for the real Jesus, who can be found only within the communities of the suffering and the abused:

> O form immaculately born,
> Betrayed a thousand times each morn,
> As many times each night denied
> Surrendered, tortured, crucified!
> Now have we seen beyond degree
> That love which has no boundary;
> Our eyes have looked on Calvary.[58]

Cullen's poem concludes in a manner that is similar to Du Bois' "Jesus Christ in Texas." In the death of Christ, God's power is revealed through Christ's empathic identification with the outcast, exposing the white-centered, white supremacists as foes of God.

Cullen's "The Black Christ" is a unique analysis of the relationship between race and religion in the Harlem Renaissance. It is typical of Harlem Renaissance representations of Jesus that see him as a figure of theological and social triumph for the marginalized. These depictions are counternarratives to the pejorative descriptions of black humanity from the racializing worldview of white-supremacist Christianity. Like "The Black Christ," narratives of Jesus in the Harlem Renaissance demythologize the white-centered story of idealized white humanity by including black suffering within the narrative of Christ, child of God, cosufferer and redeemer.

The story of the black Christ resonated with Bonhoeffer. Years later while writing *Ethics*, Bonhoeffer claimed that in Christ "we see humanity as humanity that is accepted, borne, loved, and reconciled with God. In Christ we see God in the form of our poorest brothers and sisters."[59] Jesus with the poorest of our brothers and sisters denotes Jesus within the community of those who suffer.[60] Participation in the will of God as demonstrated in Christ is defined by vicarious and empathic solidarity with the oppressed.

LEARNING FROM ALAIN LOCKE, AND THE
ECUMENICAL CONFERENCE

Bonhoeffer's incarnational investigation into the problem of race helped to further develop his theology and his interpretation of Christ-centered faithfulness. Bonhoeffer submersed himself in the Harlem Renaissance literary movement during his investigation, and he even met some of the writers. He described a visit to his classmate Albert Fisher's alma mater, Howard University, in November of his first semester at Union.[61] At the time of that visit, one of the main architects of the Harlem Renaissance, Alain Locke, was chair of the philosophy department at Howard. About that visit Bonhoeffer claimed, "I was introduced not only to the leaders of the young Negro movement at Howard College in Washington, but also in Harlem, the Negro quarter in New York."[62] Through literature and in-person encounters with writers, Bonhoeffer was intent on learning as much as he could as quickly as possible.

During his visit to Washington with Fisher, Bonhoeffer attended an ecumenical meeting and was introduced among the participants of the gathering as "a guest from Germany."[63] Bethge describes Bonhoeffer as unenthusiastic about the ecumenical and theological aspects of the gathering, but he was impressed by their passage of a resolution on the question of war guilt. The group sought to send a message to Christians in Germany to let them know that they rejected the theory agreed upon by the Allies at the Versailles Peace Conference that Germany alone should shoulder sole guilt for the war.[64] The impact of that experience for Bonhoeffer stayed with him and helped to loosen the grip of *Volk*-centeredness on him. It also influenced his ecumenical focus when he returned to Germany. Bonhoeffer's experience of that ecumenical conference in America was behind his bitter response to Emmanuel Hirsch and Paul Althaus when, in 1931, they claimed that participants in the ecumenical movement were "unpatriotic internationalists."[65] The combination of experiences in Bonhoeffer's exposure to God hidden in the suffering black Christ included a revelation of the theological necessity of peacemaking and ecumenism.

W.E.B. DU BOIS VERSUS BOOKER T. WASHINGTON

Bonhoeffer's exposure to black suffering exposed him to a public dispute among leadership in the black community. Bonhoeffer esteemed Du Bois over Booker T. Washington in the very public disagreement between the two black leaders concerning the best means of overcoming race oppression:

> B. T. Washington preaches the gospel of working, with regard to the white people separate like the fingers and one like the hand. Du Bois criticizes Washington sharply, accuses W. to agree with the statement of the inferiority of the black race. More race-proud![66]

His emphasis on Du Bois' race pride is affirming it. That is not surprising, given what he came to learn about the reception of Washington's perspective within the communities of young participants in the Harlem Renaissance, among whom he was gathering friendships at Howard and in Harlem. Some African Americans interpreted black leaders who succumbed to Washington's submission-to-racism perspective to be pawns of white racist leadership.[67] Within the black community at Abyssinian Baptist, in classes at Union, and on campus at Howard, Bonhoeffer learned about the Washington/Du Bois dispute as a contest for the value of black life and the role of black leadership in America. The elder brother of Cullen's black Christ represented this intraracial dispute as a theological argument. When Christianity offers acceptance rather than resistance to injustice, it becomes sycophantic to white racism and a theological justification of black subhumanity. Sycophantic Christianity is little more than a metaphorical painkiller in a society that is psychologically, intellectually, and physically violent toward black people. Bonhoeffer interpreted young blacks to be leaving Christianity in general because they saw it as kowtowing to white supremacy and functioning as an opiate to make African Americans acquiesce to their harsh fate in a racist society.

The combination of exposure to the Harlem literary movement and the ecumenical conference is further evidence for the influence that Bonhoeffer's time in Harlem had on his Christian development from 1930 to 1931. That year opened him to joining into the culture of an oppressed people, moving Bonhoeffer well beyond the limitations of German nationalism. The practice of joining in with African Americans in Harlem gave Bonhoeffer the ability to see more clearly the distinction between a damaging theology of glory, represented by a white Christ who refuses incarnation and empathy, and the healthier theology of the cross that reveals the presence of God hidden in suffering.

THE LOST ESSAY

After his second semester, Bonhoeffer described his New Negro experience in his report about his second semester to his church federation, borrowing the veil imagery popularized by Du Bois: "here one gets to see something of the real face of America, something that is hidden *behind the veil* of words in the American constitution saying that 'all men are created equal.' "[68] He had become familiar with New Negro literature. In a letter to Reinhold Niebuhr, written from Germany in 1933, Bonhoeffer asked him to "put in a good word" for his cousin, Hans Christoph von Hase, who had applied for a scholarship to Union. Von Hase was a pastor, and Bonhoeffer claimed that time at Union would be very good for him. At the conclusion of that letter, he asked that Niebuhr "please pass along hearty greetings to my friends from that time [in 1930–1931], particularly Jim Dobrowski (whom I ask to return my essay on Negro literature that he must still have)."[69] Bonhoeffer was a thorough scholar; his having written an essay on that literature means he had read the literature. The impact of that literature on him, and the location of his encounter with it, was undoubtedly transformative for him.

CHAPTER FOUR

CHRIST, EMPATHY, AND CONFRONTATION AT ABYSSINIAN BAPTIST CHURCH

Bonhoeffer found Harlem to be the center of an international world of radical black reimaging. Intellectuals of the Harlem Renaissance interpreted black life in a racist world with depictions of Jesus that demonstrated the hypocrisy of a Christian world-view organized by white supremacy. But the intellectuals of the Harlem Renaissance were not his only formative influences there. Bonhoeffer became a lay leader at Abyssinian Baptist Church, where he encountered a tradition of Jesus and a communal experience that stressed attention to concrete historical realities and gave him a model for *Stellvertretung*, the coordination of all of life under the gospel.

THE GERMAN TEACHER IN THE SUNDAY SCHOOL

Church life was central to Bonhoeffer's experience of Harlem. He and Albert Fisher worked together as ministry leaders with a group of boys in an afternoon Sunday school at the church. Bonhoeffer wrote of his role in the Sunday school, but he also described his involvement in some of the other ministries offered to the Harlem community at Abyssinian. To his black Baptist pastor, Adam Clayton Powell Sr., Bonhoeffer was "a German teacher in the Sunday School" whose leadership role in the church was indicative of Powell's efforts at racial reconciliation.[1] And, as a temporary lay leader at Abyssinian, Bonhoeffer was learning from Powell's ecclesiology by participating in it:

> For more than six months, I was in one of the large Baptist churches in Harlem every Sunday at 2:30 in the afternoon, and together with my friend [Albert Fisher], and often as his substitute, had a group of young Negroes in the Sunday school; I conducted Bible study for some Negro women and once a week helped out in a weekday church school. Hence not only did I become well acquainted with several young Negroes; I also visited their homes several times. This personal acquaintance with Negroes was one of the most important and gratifying events of my stay in America.[2]

Paul Lehmann writes that Bonhoeffer spent the majority of his social life in Harlem during his short time in America: "the Negro community in Harlem was at the centre of his social exploration of the country to which he had just come."[3] Lehmann claimed Bonhoeffer thoroughly interrogated the African American experience "to its minute details through books and countless visits to Harlem, through participation in Negro youth work, but even more through a remarkable kind of identity with the Negro community so that he was received there as though he had never been an outsider at all."[4] Lehmann's observations shed light on Bonhoeffer's descriptions of his time in Harlem, when church life put him in contact with the understanding of the sacred for a community of African Americans in a period of transition and crisis.

Powell's black Baptist sensibilities saw social and political action on behalf of the oppressed as a sacred and core Christian social responsibility. African American Christianity, as Bonhoeffer experienced it at Abyssinian, provided context for the development of a type of dialectical theology. There he encountered an African American interpretation of the immanent yet transcendent God, which helped to inspire the German teacher in the Sunday school to push back against injustice in simple obedience to Christ.

THE MENTAL GRID

Collectively, Harlem shared in a global experience of racialization that filtered their communal interpretations of salvation and redemption according to the social positioning of black people in a white racist world. Theology at Abyssinian was developed within communal circumstances that provided Bonhoeffer with new sources to make sense of life. Some scholars describe a "mental grid" as a complex process of filtering all of our learning through the experience of our social identity.[5] Theologically the mental grid includes one's social environment in the process of determining individual or communal ways of knowing God. Bonhoeffer's experience of learning in Harlem was unique, as it required the modification of filters formed in Germany through which he was accustomed to seeing the world and understanding himself in it. For modification to happen, Bonhoeffer had to allow himself to be vulnerable to seeing himself and society from the perspective of others, just as discipleship to the empathic and vicarious *Stellvertretung* Christ whom he described in his two dissertations required. Paul Lehmann says that Bonhoeffer did practice empathy and even seemed naturally disposed to seeing society from the perspective of others:

> His aristocracy was unmistakable yet not obtrusive. . . . [He believed one must develop] the capacity to see oneself and the world from another perspective other than one's own. This paradox of birth and nationality in Bonhoeffer has seemed to me increasingly during the years since to have made him an exciting and conspicuous example of triumph over parochialism of every kind.[6]

Bonhoeffer was a white aristocrat, a theologian, and a junior faculty member at the University of Berlin. But identity did not prevent his entering into Abyssinian as an engaged learner. By practicing empathy in Harlem, he opened himself to exploring and revising the way he saw the world from within a community that was foreign to him.

EMPATHY AND THE MENTAL GRID

Black liberation theologians agree that racial oppression plays a formative role in the black experience in America.[7] Delores Williams analyzes the theological influence of race oppression as an all-encompassing reality with four active components: a horizontal encounter, a vertical encounter, a transformation of consciousness, and an epistemological process. Her analysis demonstrates the contextual nature of all learning about God.

The horizontal encounter refers to the social interaction between black and white people. Social conditions in a white racist environment have not historically been welcoming for blacks, locally or globally. Bonhoeffer became familiar with the black/white American encounter in the south and wrote home about the treatment he observed blacks receiving from whites:

> The separation of whites from blacks in the southern states really does make a rather shameful impression. In railways that separation extends to even the tiniest details. . . . The way the southerners talk about Negroes is simply repugnant, and in this regard the pastors are no better than the others. . . . It is a bit unnerving that in a country with so inordinately many slogans about brotherhood, peace, and so on, such things continue completely uncorrected.[8]

Bonhoeffer wrote those observations on January 2, 1931, to his brother Karl Friedrich while traveling back to New York from Cuba.[9] On the heels of his encounters with racism in the south, Bonhoeffer continued to learn about lynching in America.[10] He was writing his observations of black social oppression and suffering while he was reading black writers in Harlem and serving in ministry at Abyssinian.

The vertical encounter describes the interpretation of God by the oppressed, which can be the catalyst for creative, culturally derived resources for survival. Some writers describe this encounter as the power of God providing creative possibilities in a noncreative situation.[11] African American spirituals are an example of the life-sustaining creativity of black religion in the midst of obscene cruelty. Howard Thurman describes spirituals as expressions of an African American conviction that saw life holistically, containing a series of meaning-making moments in which harsh realities in cruel environments were acknowledged and met with the hope that the resources of God's grace were not exhausted by man's inhumanity to man and that "the environment, with all its cruelty, would not crush."[12]

Bonhoeffer made references to the "Negro Spirituals," or "folksongs,"[13] that he regarded as "some of the greatest artistic achievements in America,"[14] with their "strange mixture of reserved melancholy and eruptive joy."[15] Bethge indicated that, in addition to collecting publications of the NAACP, reading a great deal of African American literature, and writing an essay on that literature while he was in Harlem, Bonhoeffer "began to collect gramophone records of spirituals, which he used five years later to introduce his students to this world which was practically unknown at the time."[16]

A transformation of consciousness describes one's self-appraisal in light of the horizontal and vertical encounters. When blacks understand God to contradict the negative messages of black humanity in a racist society and are capable of deflecting ideology that would otherwise distort their reality and diminish their self-worth, their consciousness can be understood to have undergone a positive transformation. A negative transformation of consciousness is the simultaneous forfeiture of positive black self-assessment and internalization of distorted, racist depictions of God and of black people. This is an infection of self-loathing, spread by exposure to white racism that is carried as a parasite within modern colonial strains of a contaminated white Christian worldview. The result is an oppressed person's diseased Christian imagination.

The Harlem Renaissance was a communal transformation of consciousness. Intellectuals and clergy like Powell sought a positive transformation of consciousness by articulating a healthier Jesus and exposing the hypocrisy of racist Christianity in an epistemological process. With Powell, it was unthinkable that blacks would turn from Christianity to reject racist domination and oppression; the gospel had necessarily been distorted to make it a threat to justice and to a positive transformation of consciousness. Powell understood Christian discipleship to include a this-world pursuit of justice: "therefore, do not ask what we shall eat or what we shall drink or wherewithal we shall be clothed, but seek ye first the enforcement of the Constitution and its rightness and all these things shall be added unto you."[17] For Powell, Christ was their singular advocate for justice and the catalyst for a healthier transformation of consciousness.

Attention to the first two encounters and the transformation of consciousness confers critical insight about the epistemological process that informs theology and Christian identity. Questions arise about the kinds of transformations that occur in the epistemological process, such as how social encounters inform self-understanding and how interpretations of Christ inform and are informed by social perceptions of humanity. The epistemological process reveals that all learning is socially informed and influenced by multiple sources working together in a holistic process of knowledge acquisition. That is to say, we are social, embodied people, and our learning occurs in local, social, embodied ways. By recognizing the situated, localized nature of learning, we gain a better understanding of the various life-factors that shape it and we equip people who are not members of the same formative communities to recognize the social value of empathy and to interact in healthier ways. Understanding this process helps us to appreciate what occurred in Bonhoeffer's faith transformation in Harlem: his understanding of Christ continued to develop as he gathered new information for his own epistemological process by empathically entering the epistemological process of others.

FROM THE FIELD TO THE FACTORY

From the turn of the twentieth century until well into the 1930s, Harlem was the location of an explosive and dynamic black epistemological process. Abyssinian Baptist Church was an important component of that experience. Powell and his predecessors at Abyssinian were responding as pastors to a revolutionary time in African American history. The impact of the revolutionary moment was more pronounced during and immediately following World War I, when the black American population was radically rearranging itself within the western and northern United States as throngs of people flowed like rivers away from the south.

The radical rearranging is what Isabel Wilkerson describes in her award-winning book, *The Warmth of Other Suns: The Epic Story of America's Great Migration.*[18] Prior to Bonhoeffer's Sloane Fellowship, two sizeable waves of the migration occurred as southern blacks made their way to Harlem.[19] The first wave picked up intensity during the spring of 1916 and slowed with the return of European immigrant workers and the economic downturn after World War I.[20] Before the Treaty of Versailles was signed in 1919, more than four hundred thousand African Americans left their homes in the south.[21] The second wave began around the fall of 1921 and continued with intermittent strength until the beginning of the Great Depression.[22] Powell claimed that these waves brought at least one hundred thousand migrants to New York, with most going to Harlem.[23] Carter G. Woodson was writing

A Century of Negro Migration during the first wave, and in it he echoed Powell when he claimed that whether they were runaway slaves or what Du Bois called the "talented tenth"[24] black migrants had assigned religious significance to the north for centuries, seeing it as a promised land.[25]

The Great Migration connected religious significance to racial uplift for African Americans. Combined with slavery and emancipation, it contributed to the horizontal and vertical encounters that shaped an African American consciousness. The horizontal influence was both social and economic, as one author explains in the *Negro Year Book* for 1918–1919:

> No event since the emancipation of the Negroes from slavery so profoundly influenced the economic and social life of the Negro. It may be said that whereas the Thirteenth Amendment granted physical emancipation, the conditions brought about by World War I made for the economic emancipation of the Negro, in that he found for the first time opportunity to go practically anywhere in the United States and find employment along a great many lines, many of which had hitherto [been] closed entirely to him.[26]

Migrant blacks headed north during World War I for job opportunities, to be free from Jim Crow segregation and from fear of violent white racism. In 1910, 89 percent of African Americans lived in the south, but ten years later that number was reduced by more than 5 percent.[27] Woodson recognized that the bulk of the African American population was choosing to remain in the south, but, as Wilkerson describes, the Great Migration saw enormous numbers of black southerners leave the land of their forefathers in the biggest underreported story of the century, heading toward "an uncertain existence in nearly every other corner of America."[28] The population of migrating blacks was large enough to plunder a particularly valuable labor force and disrupt the southern economy.

THE BLACK EXODUS TO BETTER EXPLOITATION

Because of the Great War, a thinner northern labor force was eager for their arrival. Blacks became a surrogate labor source, replacing poor whites and European immigrants who, prior to the war, had been the preferred supply of cheap labor by northern industry. That labor source was reduced by immigration restrictions and would-be immigrants deciding to stay home to help defend their country in the midst of the outbreak the Great War.[29] And during the war, black migrants in the north found themselves surprisingly well received, even sought after, in those very places that had previously shunned them:

> Women of color formerly excluded from domestic service by foreign maids are now in demand. Many mills and factories which Negroes were prohibited from entering a few years ago are now bidding for their labor. Railroads cannot find help to keep their property in repair, contractors fall short of their plans for failure to hold mechanics drawn into the industrial boom and the United States Government has had to advertise for men to hasten the preparation for war.[30]

Labor was a major part of the birth of black urban life. The wages that black migrants received in munitions plants, railroad construction, stockyards, and factories far exceeded what they knew in the south. Pay of seventy-five cents a day on a southern farm paled in comparison to the $3.00 and sometimes $4.00 per day in a northern factory. Female domestic workers could expect $1.50 to $3.00 per week in the south, while in the urban north they could expect $2.50 per day.[31] By the time of Bonhoeffer's arrival to Harlem in 1930, the numbers of blacks living in Harlem topped 165,000 in living spaces packed so densely that many tenants had to sleep in shifts; as soon as one person awoke and went off to work, someone else filled the vacant bed.[32] But, in spite of the conditions, they were hopeful; Jim Crow, lynching, and humiliation behind them, higher wages, better schools, and perhaps even cohumanity before them, the black exodus was saturated with hope and religious significance.

THE SOUTHERN MIGRANT'S DREAM DEFERRED IN HARLEM

But they soon discovered that the north was not a promised land of milk and honey. Migrants settled down in poorer sections of their destination cities only to meet struggle and conflicts with white neighbors and white workers, usually of immigrant background.[33] Frictions arose between blacks and working-class whites as blacks entered competition for jobs, looked for available housing, and were used by industry leaders to break strikes. The frictions that erupted in the postwar north were both racist and classist in structure. Racial discord between the working classes was the result of economic factors, especially job competition; leadership within the economic power base that was bent on maintaining dominance cultivated racial discord. Racism worked to undermine the well-being and objective interests of white and black workers alike.[34] Blacks and whites together could have been a potent force for positive changes in labor, but blacks were isolated in the labor force and were often employed as scabs, crossing picket lines during disputes between corporate elites and the labor unions that often excluded black workers. In that precarious employment arrangement, blacks were much more vulnerable than poor whites.[35] In addition to being shunned by labor unions, blacks were crowded into poor neighborhoods and forced to live in dilapidated and unsanitary buildings with high rents.[36] Powell argued that blacks were segregated into poor-quality schools and paid much less than whites for the same work:

> Color prejudice not only sees that the Negro is confined to unskilled labor, regardless of his qualifications, but it makes sure that he does not receive the same compensation that other men receive for the same work. An employment agency on Sixth Avenue in New York displayed one day the following notices on its bulletin board: "*An elevator boy wanted—Colored; hours 8a.m. to 8p.m. daily, $65 dollars per month. Elevator boy wanted—White; hours 8 a.m. to 7 p.m. daily, $90 per month.*" Even in New York it costs an elevator man 365 hours extra labor and $300 a year to be colored. . . . This is not the end of the story. The white elevator man in New York pays twenty-five percent less house rent than the colored elevator man.[37]

The race problem in New York accentuated the class problem. An economic recession immediately followed World War I, and blacks were subjected to the last hired, first fired policy, only deepening the hard-hitting impact of a difficult economy.[38] The environment was an unhealthy one, psychologically and physically, as Cheryl Lynn Greenberg explains: "Poverty, overcrowding, and poor housing conditions led to startlingly high illness rates and mortality rates. Black rates of malnutrition, disease, and death far exceeded white."[39]

Black migrants also navigated a different moral environment within black inner-city neighborhoods as participants in the birth of the oppressed, black urban community. The plight of the black migrant in the urban north after World War I signaled the dawn of the poor inner-city black neighborhood, in the context of what

Langston Hughes described as "a dream deferred."[40] The Great Migration brought blacks to Harlem, hopeful and dreaming of a promised land, to meet disappointment and despair. In their despair, they collectively turned to the black church as their help and familiar center of the community.

ABYSSINIAN BAPTIST CHURCH MOVES
TO HARLEM

When Rev. Adam Clayton Powell Sr. became the pastor of Abyssinian Baptist Church, it was located in lower Manhattan on Fortieth Street, between Seventh and Eighth Avenues, in its third building since its founding in 1808. Shortly after he assumed leadership there, Powell realized that Abyssinian must move to Harlem.[41] He was not the first pastor of Abyssinian to reach that conclusion. In 1901, one of his predecessors, Reverend R. D. Wynn, was so convinced that the church should be in Harlem that he resigned after a sixteen-year pastorate when the congregation refused. The following year, in 1902, Dr. C. S. Morris succeeded Wynn and was able to convince the church, but in six years Morris got the church to move only as far as Fortieth Street from its location at Waverly Place before he, too, succumbed to frustration and resigned.[42] Powell took the helm on New Year's Eve, 1908. He agreed with his predecessors that Harlem was where Abyssinian needed to relocate and began the push in that direction. Powell's brand of pastoral leadership and ministry focus was different from that of his predecessors, and as a result, the future location of the church was inevitable; under the leadership of the stalwart Powell, Abyssinian opened its doors for dedication in Harlem at 138th Street, between Lennox and Seventh Avenue, on May 20, 1923. It had taken 115 years and the resignation of three pastors, including Powell Sr., before the congregation surrendered to the unavoidable, begged Powell to retake the helm, and moved into Harlem.

ADAM CLAYTON POWELL SR. AND THE ATTITUDE
OF THE NEGRO CHURCH TOWARD
THE SOUTHERN MIGRATION

On July 1, 1917, during the apex of a major wave of migration, Abyssinian was still located on Fortieth Street in lower

Manhattan. At 3:00 that afternoon, the church held a mass meeting, and Powell spoke on the topic of the attitude of the Negro church toward southern migration. That year, Powell traveled to destination sites for the migration "through the southern and western states to Los Angeles, Cal. and back"[43] to investigate "the cyclone-like movement" that in less than twelve months had brought large numbers of blacks from the south and plundered the southern economy.[44] With no clear leader of the movement, blacks were fatigued with the poor leadership that they were subject to, and en masse they sought to help themselves. As Powell explained, "The colored people have become disgusted with the leadership of cornstalk preachers, weak-kneed professors, and spineless politicians. Their progress has been impeded by too much of this kind of leadership."[45]

Powell's reference to spineless politicians was an indication of his early disagreement with Booker T. Washington, who argued that the racist rural south was the better, and natural, environment for blacks.[46] For Powell, Washington's rhetoric did not match the reality of southern black life. Indeed, many blacks viewed Washington's perspective as an illustration of *Old Negro* accommodationism: a sycophantic, conciliatory approach to southern white racists by blacks who have assimilated a white-supremacist worldview by virtue of a negative transformation of consciousness. Religion was appealed to by blacks in the assimilationist approach as strongly eschatological "pie-in-the-sky" worship or as a misinterpretation of Jesus' commandment to "turn the other cheek" as a permissive approach to social evil.

Powell's approach to the migrant's plight was not to advocate accommodation to racism but to amplify protest. Powell understood the church to be responsible for meeting the migrants in their crisis, with hope.[47]

HOLISTIC MINISTRY AND THE PROBLEM OF STATUS INCONSISTENCY

Powell initially struggled to get his church to pay attention to the plight of the migrants. He urged the congregation of Abyssinian to recognize their Christian responsibility to the new arrivals in Harlem, at least for the sake of their family members who were counted among the throng of southern migrants. As Powell argued,

"There was hardly a member in Abyssinian Church who could not count one or more relatives among the new arrivals."[48] For Powell, the role of the model church in Harlem matched the role that the black church traditionally held in the black community north and south. The church was traditionally the center of black social life and the foundation for organized life in African American communities.[49] Albert Fisher knew that to be true as well, growing up in a family of black Baptist preachers.

Yet some black-church scholars argue that migrating blacks found black-church membership to be an impediment to attaining middle-class economic status.[50] Accordingly, they embraced Booker T. Washington's model of assimilation to a racist worldview to identify with mainstream white culture and to shed what was interpreted as folkloric, pejorative blackness. If these black church scholars are correct, the assimilationist perspective in his church may account for Powell's struggle to convince his congregation to care for the plight of the migrants.

Most of the members of Abyssinian were middle class. Although they were a black congregation, they were financially able to buy six lots in Harlem and construct their own large church at a cost of $334,881, the equivalent of $5 million in 2013. This was paid for by church members alone while they were also contributing a significant amount of money to education within the community, a home abroad for foreign missionaries, and the 2013 equivalent of another $300,000 toward the purchase of a home for aged church members. Powell's Abyssinian Church paid those bills with tithing money, supplemented with the sale of their building on Fortieth Street. Yet, a deeper engagement with their situation in New York yields conclusions not recognized by scholars arguing an assimilationist perspective. The social obstacles that Abyssinian members faced in the larger white society were not due to their membership in a black church; rather, the struggle they faced was with status inconsistency.[51] Blacks who achieved success financially or academically, and thus an advanced social standing in some areas, desired to be recognized in society by that higher status or achieved rank. They were successful, middle-class "Negroes." Yet in their social contacts with whites in a racialized society, their desire to be recognized by their achievements was met with a vested interest in seeing them according to their lowest social rank; they were merely "Negroes," capable of nothing more than what was typically associated with black characters in a white-supremacist narrative. Even middle-class and wealthy professional black people could not escape pejorative white social implications of their blackness.

The worldview of wealthy blacks in Powell's ministry cannot be captured by the supposed struggle for assimilation. Powell's ministry perceived the role of the black church as holistically engaged in the experiences of black people, seeing the whole person under the claims of the gospel. Powell's perspective was broad enough to encompass status inconsistency within its understanding of dialectically opposed black Christian experiences and the role of church within them. Eric C. Lincoln describes this holistic process of engagement as a black dialectical ecclesiology, and it is discernable within Powell's description of the model church.

BLACK DIALECTICAL ECCLESIOLOGY

Rather than assimilating the black church out of existence for racial uplift, the black Baptist community at Abyssinian demonstrated a historical engagement with dialectically opposed social tensions in their Christian experience. Powell's ecclesiology was not new; Lincoln argues that black church communities in general, like that of Abyssinian, practiced a holistic engagement with the sacred in everyday living.[52] Bonhoeffer heard this engagement as a "strange mixture of melancholy hope" within the black spirituals of his admiration. Hence, status inconsistency was not a new reality for southern or northern churchgoing blacks; their Christian worldview recognized it as a part of life. Lincoln sees the black church engagement with the strange mixture that Bonhoeffer encountered as occurring in four dialectics, namely, priestly and prophetic functions, otherworldly and this-worldly tensions, universalism and particularism, and accommodation and resistance.

The dialectic between priestly and prophetic roles within the general black church describes the functions of church life as a balance between worship—with "priestly" attention to the in-group maintenance of the inner life of Christians and the church community—and the "prophetic" church involvement in the political concerns and activities of the wider community. Black churches employ both functions, but black churches are varied in their proximity to one or the other. Priestly churches are citadels of

survival that serve as a place to escape a hostile world and prophetic churches are networks of liberation that empower communities to speak truth to power.[53]

The dialectic between otherworldly and this-worldly orienta-
tions describes the tension within the perspectives of black believers toward the world. An otherworldly orientation is viewed in the
pejorative, as a pie-in-the-sky religious mentality that sees life after
death as the only source of hope in suffering and avoids engaging
political matters of fairness and justice. A this-worldly engagement emphasizes justice with a present-day focus on politics and
social matters. This dialectic resembles the priestly and prophetic
tension: a this-worldly/otherworldly dialectic refers to the way of
seeing society and one's role in it, while the priestly/prophetic dialectic pays primary attention to the function of church practices.
The two dialectical pairs are often connected in black churches in
a mixture between conservative theology and liberal politics. An
eschatological claim on this-world behavior made by a prophetic
critique of contemporary social injustice with reference to otherworldly values intertwines all four dialectical poles within these
two pairs.[54] And, consistent with a historical black ecclesiology,
Powell argued that the church as the body of Christ was the center
of community.[55] Its inner functioning (priestly/otherworldly) and
its social and political activity (prophetic/this-worldly) is ministry
described as attention given to human suffering in the name of
Christ. Powell called it "applied Christianity."[56]

Attention to the priestly/prophetic dialectic helps our understanding of Powell's politically inflected theology. Powell was a
member of the NAACP in Manhattan and one of the founding
members of the National League on Urban Conditions that was
formed in New York to help improve the social conditions of
blacks in the city.[57] These engagements hold together the various
poles within the dialectics of function and orientation. Powell's
political and social activities were the core of his theological convictions and perspectives on the role of the church.

The dialectic between universalism and particularism is
reflected by the black church's engagement with the tension
between the poles of the universality of the Christian message and
the particularity of black history.[58] Black churches emerged out of
a common experience of race-based slavery within the American

version of modern colonial Christianity. They have historically been congregations of segreg*ated* people, but blacks were not a seg-reg*ating* people; segregated worship was an imposed component of a white-supremacist social imagination. In this paradigm, most black churches have maintained a position of antiracism and open-ness to all races, typically raising the flag of racial reconciliation and the brotherhood and sisterhood of all of God's children, while confronting false universals that ignore the inconsistencies in a black Christian experience. Black churches do not share a consen-sus about how to approach the black experience of race in America, at times taking very different positions on black consciousness when faced with white racism (e.g., Booker T. Washington's soft accommodation of white racism vs. W.E.B. Du Bois' vocal resis-tance). Yet it is consistently true in black churches that worship-pers are aware that race has played an important role in the lives of black Christians. Attention to racism in the context of a universal Christian message has been a critical element of the black church's message.[59] And it was the motivation for Powell's intentionally diverse church leadership that made room for Bonhoeffer within the instructional life of the church community.[60]

Powell claimed, "Both races should realize that the man who loves is always superior to the man who hates."[61] As a matter of faith, Powell made it "one of the chief objectives of the church . . . to cultivate a more sympathetic relationship between the races," recognizing that the ability to love one another—if we are to obey Christ—depends on our ability to push past our popular intragroup characterizations of the "other" and into real knowledge of our neighbor.[62] In his autobiography, Powell quoted John D. Rockefeller, who argued, "The reason we do not love each other more is because we do not know each other better."[63] And to that end, Powell shaped a worship environment that he claimed would "help all races under-stand each other better that they might love one another more." He nurtured a diverse leadership at Abyssinian: "we had a Jew on the Usher Board, a German teacher in the Sunday School, a mixed fac-ulty in our Teacher Training School, and for several years, a white instructor for our Red Cross Nurse Training Classes." All of this was done alongside a program of "Reconciliation Trips," in which groups of whites visited Abyssinian every month to attend church and "study our social, educational, and religious program." The particular/universal black church dialectic is illustrative of a universal language that begins in the authenticity of particularity rather than in feigned objectivity.

The dialectic between resistance and accommodation is one in which the black church plays the role of mediating institution, helping blacks to be contributing members in the larger white social and political structures by brokering white cultural norms in a familiar black context. The role of brokering this mediation is distinct from assimilation. After the Civil War black churches helped former slaves accommodate to their new lives by providing the education that white supremacy had denied them. Black churches played a mediating role between slave life and freedom by equipping former slaves for independence and enabling them to be contributing members of society. Abyssinian Baptist was also a mediating institution. Powell offered an extensive program of church education for Harlem residents through Abyssinian's church and community house. Abyssinian was an institutional church; it met various needs in addition to worship and religious education.[64] The Abyssinian Baptist Church and Community House, under Powell's leadership, was very much like Charles Fisher's 16th Street Baptist Church in Birmingham, Alabama; it maintained a system of housing and land development, an employment agency, and a multidiscipline church school:

> Our School of Religious Education included teacher training classes, weekday religious education classes and five Bible classes. We were conducting classes in physical education, elementary English, citizenship and our system of government, designing and dressmaking, home nursing, typewriting and shorthand as well as a school of dramatic art directed by Richard B. Harrison of "Green Pastures" fame.[65] There were four clubs for boys and six for girls, a Thursday Community Forum led by Attorney Aaron Smith, a Sunday Evening Community Lyceum presided over by the brilliant attorney, Myrtle B. Anderson, and a Book-A-Month Club. . . . Socially minded white and colored people were coming from everywhere to see our institution and hear about its program.[66]

The programs of Abyssinian's community house met the needs of migrants by equipping them for their new environment and new opportunities in the north. Powell determined that Abyssinian Baptist would be a mediating institution for migrants needing education for a black identity away from the farm fields: "The church will be a kind of intellectual go between the public schools and the institutions of learning. Thousands of members of our race are coming to the northern cities every year, who are too old to be reached by public school and too poorly informed to enter universities."[67] Powell's effort was different from the accommodationism that Booker T. Washington came to represent. Within the black community at Abyssinian, Bonhoeffer heard the perspectives of Washington and Du Bois, and he esteemed Du Bois' black resistance model over Booker T. Washington's accommodating response to white racism.[68]

Du Bois' resistance model sought to oppose the assimilative accommodating forces of white supremacy so that the self-esteem of the marginalized black community could be preserved and even nurtured. Resistance was the mentality of the self-assured who found their identity not in the common definitions placed upon them by the dominant socio-political systems. Christ-informed resistance empowered black church communities to deflect pejorative depictions of black people from a dominant racist society and to make claims upon social and political structures for human rights and equal opportunities. Powell was also influenced by Walter Rauschenbusch's interpretation of the social gospel in his Christ-centered resistance. Powell argued that the church must "Christianize the social order" in direct reference to Rauschenbusch's popular book.[69] By this Powell meant that the church must live completely in the world in faithfulness to the Bible in daily living. To relieve the spiritual and physical needs of society, "every service rendered should give men a sense of the Fatherhood of God and the Brotherhood of man."[70] The notion of the family of humankind called to mind the same language used of God in Cullen's poem "The Black Christ" and in Du Bois' "Credo." It is a black-church understanding of humanity that served as a rampart against pejorative labels of black humanity in a Christ-centered model of resistance. Powell made this argument as well: "the Negro church is the only church that has persistently opposed lynching and the Negro pulpit is the only pulpit that has unceasingly preached the brotherhood of man."[71] Hence, the accommodation/resistance dialectic is illustrative of a black experience of the church that is empowered by a black interpretation of Christ in the context of African American survival.

ECCLESIOLOGY AS FAITHFULNESS IN ACTION

Bonhoeffer's exposure to ministry at Abyssinian was the stimulus to help capture a Christian social perspective that he would otherwise not have known as a German Lutheran. It helped him meet his goal of studying systematic theology "as it has developed under completely different circumstances."[72] He found that Powell's ecclesiology harmonized the polarities of African American life under the gospel, demonstrating the complexity of black churches as social and political institutions and their multifaceted theological stimulus for ministry. Powell's ecclesiology was driven by his interpretation of Christ: faithfulness to Christ was merely the outcome and the evidence of the life-giving presence of Christ within the believer and the believing community.

> Just as the branches receive their life from the vine, so the Christian receives their life from Christ. Without an abiding connection with Christ, the Christian is hopeless, helpless, powerless, and lifeless. . . . The Christian takes in spiritual nourishment. He feeds upon the spiritual bread and drinks the spiritual water.[73]

The intake of Christ is made manifest in our life by the export of demonstrated love of neighbor:

> Every drunkard, every street-walker, every wrecker of social conditions, is a challenge to our Christianity, not our criticism. . . . Is there anything in us that responds to the individual and social needs? We receive that we may serve. The wealth of a nation is not measured by its imports but by its exports.[74]

Hence, the evidence of Christian living is not measured by one's religious knowledge; Christian living is the outworking of one's love for God in a holistic engagement with the sacred in everyday life that is made manifest by faithfulness to Christ in social behavior.

Because of its ability to embrace all of life within the scope of God's sovereignty, Powell's ecclesiology was robust enough to deflect the incursion of popular white-supremacist dogma. The notion of the passive black Christian was problematic in Harlem, as Bonhoeffer observed, because it suggested that Christianity was merely an opiate for oppressed people. Powell saw opiate Christianity resulting from the compartmentalizing of Christianity rather than Christianity encompassing all of life. He argued that the Lordship of Christ extended over all areas of life, including especially the concrete needs of humanity in this world.

Bonhoeffer recognized the problems with a Christianity that encouraged acquiescence to oppression. During the church struggle in 1933, he tried to help his colleagues to see that compartmentalizing their faith allowed them to ignore Jewish persecution. For Bonhoeffer and Powell, fidelity to the life and ministry of Jesus depended on acknowledging life in this world and affirming that Christians should act to relieve suffering. That was, for Powell, the role of a model church. As he explained, a model church connects theological thought and daily lived experience for good stewardship on the earth. Without this connection, there can be no fidelity to Christ. This line of thinking has a very clear connection to the Bonhoeffer we know after 1931.

"A MODEL CHURCH"

On October 29, 1929, the stock market crashed, plunging the nation into the Great Depression. The impact of that crash on African Americans was devastating; by the end of 1929, three hundred thousand black laborers were out of work.[75] The first full year of the depression, 1930, saw the unemployment rate climb to 10 percent for all Americans across the country, but the application of "last hired, first fired" was in full swing for northern blacks, and the numbers of unemployed blacks in Harlem quadrupled.[76] On November 27 of that year, while Bonhoeffer was beginning to learn about the African American worldview in Harlem, Powell's inspirational sermon "A Model Church" was published in the *Watchman Examiner: A National Baptist Paper.* Harlem blacks were deep in misery. Powell's sermon was a clear articulation of his ecclesiology in a moment of crisis, as a call to action.

THE ACTS 2 MODEL IN SIX CONSTITUENTS

Powell's "model church" was rooted in his interpretation of Acts 2, which he understood to be the template for faithful Christian churches. The church in Acts "was organized by the direction of Jesus, and was vitalized by the presence of the Holy Spirit."[77] Its organization and vitalization carried with it a most salient feature for Powell: it was an active church, socially, politically, and spiritually, and it connected those arenas in a manner that was faithful to the centrality of the Lordship of Christ. It held in tension the dialectical poles with attention to Christ's leadership. Powell describes the model church systematically, in six active convictions that he saw present in the life and activity of the Acts church: conviction of sin, saving faith, stewardship, recognized responsibility, soul saving, and spirit-filled membership.

CONVICTION OF SIN

The members of the model church were convicted of their sins; conviction leads to repentance, and repentance leads one to turn from sin. Conviction is vital to the formation of Christ followers because "no one has ever turned from sin until he has felt the evil effects of sin so keenly that he cries with Isaiah, 'Woe is me for I am undone.'"[78] Conviction of sin is the first crucial step in dismantling old harmful paradigms and sinful practices. No one is exempt from the conviction of sin, neither the poor nor the socially elite. Hence, Powell does not advocate a belief in the innate goodness of humankind or the inevitable progress of humanity, like the American modern liberal theologians that Bonhoeffer encountered in New York classrooms and white congregations. Powell argues, "Man needs to be done over, but he cannot be done over until he is undone."[79] Following Christ begins with conviction, which leads to repentance as the second step in turning to God, "for it leads to saving faith in the efficacy of the atonement made by Jesus."[80] Conviction of sin and repentance disrupt the innate human condition of sin and selfishness by the in-breaking of God's grace that moves us toward the faith in Christ that saves us. This emphasis on repentance would have been new for Bonhoeffer and familiar at the same time. Powell's language of sin was new because, as Bonhoeffer would later confess, Christianity was initially for him primarily academic, but it became something very different. Yet, it was also familiar, because Powell's description of the in-breaking of God's grace was a theme that corresponded with his Barthian reading of Luther. For Bonhoeffer, Christ is the self-revelation of God who is our life that comes to us from the outside of ourselves as *Stellvertretung*. We are not self-made; we become a new humanity in Christ.

SAVING FAITH

Powell claims that faith that lacks movement toward God is merely mental ascent, not saving faith. One can hear echoes of Bonhoeffer's admonition against cheap grace in Powell's claims about saving faith. Powell declares that faith demands a response to Christ; without conviction of sin and repentance, faith does not move one toward God and is not saving faith. Mere mental ascent or an intellectual religion does not save us. Rather, movement toward God is demonstrated by an active faith, and Powell feared that the resistance that he saw in the church to an active response to needy migrants demonstrated more mental ascent to creeds than saving faith in Christ: "I fear there are many people in our churches who have only an intellectual religion. To believe in God with the head is simply to give mental ascent to the truths of the Bible and mental ascent does not save."[81] Conviction of sin and repentance moves one to saving faith, which is faith in action.

Saving faith is faith in Christ. For Powell, it is unequivocal; faith in Christ means simple obedience to Christ's commandments: "The best definition I know of saving faith is the statement made by the mother of Jesus to the waiters in Canaan of Galilee when the wine gave out: 'Whatsoever he saith unto you do it.' Faith consists more in doing than it does in believing."[82] Bonhoeffer would later declare in *Discipleship*, "The disciple's answer is not a spoken confession of faith in Jesus. It is the obedient deed."[83] Powell and the post–New York Bonhoeffer emphasized the concreteness of discipleship in a discernable connection between faith and everyday living.

CHRISTIAN STEWARDSHIP

Stewardship in a model church is a practiced investment in one another that demonstrates our care for each other. The model church is a caring community that recognizes itself as stewarding God's resources. What we possess is not our own; it belongs to God. Hence, it must also belong to those whom God loves. "God not only owns the great universe, but every man and woman belongs to him by creation, and every Christian is his by redemption. . . . Stewardship implies ownership and ownership involves responsibility."[84] We are penultimate facilitators of God's resources, and we must one day give account of how we use them. Christian stewardship is Christian responsibility to act in accordance with the love of God for our neighbors.

RECOGNIZED RESPONSIBILITY

In Acts 2 members of the first church recognized the responsibility given to them by God as stewards of what God owned. "They simply recognized themselves as agents through whom God met the needs of men and women."[85] The church must recognize its responsibility to act in accordance with the love of God for creation and to meet the needs of the community. A model church meets physical needs as well as spiritual ones:

> It is just as much our duty to get men and women positions during this unemployment depression, as it is to get them into church. . . . A man hungry and cold will not have much patience with a lecture on spirituality. . . . Every New Testament church must find the real needs of the people in the community in which it is located and do its utmost to supply those needs in the name and in the spirit of the Lord Jesus.[86]

A model church recognizes its responsibility to steward God's resources in faithful obedience to Christ by meeting the concrete needs of its neighbors. This admonition remained with Bonhoeffer and is evident upon his return to Germany in his care for a confirmation class that he taught for a group of boys in Berlin's Prenzlauer Berg district, a poor working-class neighborhood in east Berlin, where he also sought to become a pastor. It was also with him in a youth club that he helped start in Charlottenburg, which was another poor neighborhood where Bonhoeffer gave himself to the ministry of poverty relief prior to the church struggle in Germany. Powell's admonition about Christian responsibility provided a Christ-centered interpretation of community among the socially marginalized that helped to develop Bonhoeffer's sense of the Christian community and impacted the way he understood what the church should be doing when the church struggle began in 1933.

SOUL-SAVING, SPIRIT-FILLED MEMBERSHIP

The model church is a soul-saving church, not a social club, and it is one in that its members are infused with the life of God—the Holy Spirit—for action. "Just as the sap life rises in the tree and pushes off the dead leaves, makes it to bud, bloom and bring forth fruit, so the Holy Spirit rises in the life of a spiritually dead man changing all [of] his thoughts and acts. A church without the Holy Spirit is like a tree without sap."[87] Evidence of a Spirit-filled church is its activity; a live one is active, doing the work of God to relieve suffering in the community where it is located. A dead one does not concern itself with such things.

Powell's message was clear: the church as portrayed in Acts 2 is the model for the formation and maintenance of a faithful Christian community. According to the model, a Christian church is a community of people whose love for God compels them to faithful engagement with the world. He concludes the sermon by asking, "Is there such a church on earth?"[88] Bonhoeffer left Germany for his Sloane Fellowship in New York asking the same question about a church that would demonstrate his understanding of Christ existing as the church community. Powell seems to offer a similar Christ-centered message. But with Powell there is a strong social and political commentary: faithful stewardship of God's resources requires recognizing the pre-eminence of Christ and that, in obedience to Christ, God's people are called to action to relieve suffering. Christian virtue is not only an internal condition; it is also politically and socially a source of hope in the pursuit of freedom and justice. A Christian and her church must do more than clarify creeds and theology within the Christian community; a faithful representation of the gospel of Jesus Christ occurs in a community of obedient believers who act to engage the world, demonstrating their creeds by their deeds.

THE GREAT DEPRESSION IN HARLEM

Pastor Adam Clayton Powell Sr. liked to use the language of "creeds and deeds." For Powell, the call to demonstrate creeds was not only for laypeople; he publicly demanded that church leaders demonstrate their creeds in the life they lived and in the causes of their church. In December 1930, at the end of the first semester of Bonhoeffer's Sloane Fellowship and the first full year of the Great Depression, Powell engaged pastors in Harlem in a "creeds and deeds" church struggle over the responsibility of black-church leadership for the plight of blacks suffering in the Great Depression. The meeting was very contentious and would prove to be, in his words, "the most disappointing and discouraging chapter in my long public career."[89]

By the end of November 1930, Powell recognized that blacks in Harlem were "facing their hardest winter since emancipation."[90] The nation had abandoned the African American community, its most hard-hit population, and from all appearances black leaders were guilty of doing the same. During the first week of December 1930, Nannie H. Burroughs published a syndicated article in which she challenged black leadership in every organization, "including the preachers and the churches," to stop neglecting the condition of blacks:

> What on earth is the matter with Negro organizations—Church, Fraternal, Welfare and Educational, National and State—that they are so impotent in the present economic crisis and industrial depression? The people are out of work; they are hungry . . . they are like sheep without a shepherd. Where are the leaders? . . . What can the leaders do about it? They can do a great deal about it if they care a great deal about it. . . . Religion isn't worth a cent if it does not give you overcoming faith. . . . It is time for men who represent God to speak.[91]

Powell read this and was moved with compassion. Burrough's rebuke revealed the apathetic and compartmentalized pie-in-the-sky Christianity within the black church community. Powell waited for a written response from other New York clergy, and in the absence of a response from black clergy, "for fear that silence may be construed as giving consent"[92] to the do-nothing attitude that Burroughs castigated, Powell the bellicose social gospel advocate went on the offensive.

He did not defend himself or other black clergymen. Powell added a clergyman's voice to Burrough's complaint by "breaking into the columns of every Negro newspaper in the United States" with rebuke.[93] His response went further than hers to describe the blight caused by the depression in the black community, drawing on his access to information provided by the National Urban League to illustrate his point:

> About two weeks ago . . . T. Arnold Hill of the National Urban League, completed and published a survey of "Unemployment Among Negroes" in the United States. This report shows that about one fourth of the colored people in the twenty-five large cities are out of work and hungry. This is not only a most pathetic challenge to every race leader and race organization, but every Negro individual who has a job and is living comfortably. If the churches do not answer this challenge they ought to shut up and close up.[94]

Powell's public critique set off a powder keg in the black church community. He figured that "since Jesus and the apostles led the world in caring for the poor and needy, I thought it was proper and right that my plea should be made chiefly to the clergymen and churches of all denominations."[95] But his appeal was not welcomed as an insider's concern for the family of faith; many black clergymen interpreted Powell's public admonition as "cheap notoriety" and a successful attempt to injure the ministry of fellow black clergy.[96] Powell intended his reproach as provocation that he hoped it would lead clergy to pay attention to the needs of the suffering poor in Harlem. Instead the clergy returned his critique with some of their own, interpreting Powell's criticism as an inside attack on the black church community.

THE ENCOUNTER WITH CHRIST HIDDEN IN SUFFERING

But Powell saw himself as an advocate for "suffering humanity."[97] Powell understood Christ to be present in the encounter we have with the suffering of the needy.[98] For Powell, Christians must not be complacent or apathetic in this encounter, for to do so would be to ignore the very presence and needs of Christ.

Three weeks before Powell wrote his contentious public appeal, he was mobilizing his church to relieve suffering in service to Christ. Just prior to his Christmas trip to Cuba, Bonhoeffer was most likely hearing "the genuine proclamation of the gospel from a Negro"[99] at Abyssinian when Powell preached two consecutive Sunday sermons, the first Sunday entitled "A Naked God" and the next one "A Hungry God." Powell indicated that the suffering and destitute population of Harlem was a constant subject of his prayers, and his lament to God for the poor returned to him as a directive from God: "I kept praying to God to clothe the naked and feed the poor, but I could not get rid of the words, 'Ye clothed me—ye fed me.'" The reference was to Matthew 25, which became for him a public appeal: "if we fail to do this [give help to the poor] we should never again preach or read from the twenty-fifth chapter of Matthew—'I was hungry and ye fed me; I was naked and ye clothed me.'"[100] Bonhoeffer would later make similar admonitions during the confessing church movement in Germany on behalf of the Jews, declaring, "Only he who cries out for the Jews can sing the Gregorian chant."[101] Christians must not ignore the naked, hungry black casualties of the Great Depression. Responsible Christian service recognizes that any help given to "the least of these" is serving Christ.

Powell accompanied his words of rebuke with action. When he preached "A Hungry God," he pledged four months of his own salary toward Abyssinian's Unemployment Relief Fund, to aid in the suffering caused by the depression. The combination of his inspiring sermons and his personal sacrifice aroused the congregation to give abundantly: "before I could finish delivery of the sermon, the audience was rushing forward placing money on the table to feed 'a hungry God.' One woman left her pocketbook containing her week's wages and walked home."[102] Powell's sermons generated $2,500 in donations from his congregation,[103] all of which went to fund the "largest relief bureau ever set up by colored people."[104] Adam Clayton Powell Jr., who was at the time a student at Union Seminary with Bonhoeffer, organized and directed Abyssinian's relief effort, which included a free food kitchen, a clothing giveaway, and an employment agency.[105] By the end of Bonhoeffer's Sloane Fellowship year, Abyssinian Baptist had served nearly thirty thousand free meals, sent out 525 baskets containing more than two thousand free dinners, and distributed nearly eighteen thousand pieces of clothing and two thousand pairs of shoes.[106]

THE CONCLUSION OF THE FELLOWSHIP

Bonhoeffer's Sloane Fellowship ended in June 1931. By the time he boarded the ship to return home to Germany, much had changed for him. Bonhoeffer claimed that his philosophy and theology were revived through new perspectives he encountered in New York.[107]

Working in ministry at Abyssinian during the Harlem Renaissance was a key factor in his revival during his overall experience as a Sloane Fellow at Union Theological Seminary.

Bonhoeffer was exposed to an African American Christian worldview in Harlem while Harlem was ground zero for the rebirth of the narrative of humanity on the underside of the color line. By the time of his return to Germany, Bonhoeffer was also a veteran of trips to Mexico, Cuba, and various places throughout the southern United States, all spaces where his practice of empathic entering inspired learning from different contexts. His time in Harlem, Washington, and the southern United States made him a witness of the "Negro problem" in American Christianity, through personal relationships and through literature.[108] By the time he returned to Germany, Bonhoeffer was a year older and much wiser.

BONHOEFFER'S TRANSFORMED ECCLESIOLOGY IN NEW YORK: A CONCRETE GOSPEL FOR SUFFERING

The tradition of Jesus the cosufferer hidden in suffering and shame that Bonhoeffer encountered within Powell's ministry and within the Harlem Renaissance literary movement remained with him when he returned home. In 1932 Bonhoeffer was an ordained chaplain at the technical college in Charlottenburg, Berlin. Not quite a full year after he returned from his Sloane Fellowship, on May 29, Bonhoeffer preached a sermon from Luke 16:19-31 about the rich man and Lazarus and the need for Christian attention to suffering. Bonhoeffer argued that the gospel of Christ must be understood in concrete terms to encompass all of life. The gospel is distorted when it is compartmentalized to the spiritual life alone:

> One cannot understand and preach the gospel concretely [*handgrei-flich*] enough. . . . [But] we have spiritualized the gospel—that is, we have lightened it up, changed it. Take our gospel of the rich man and poor Lazarus. It has become a common practice to see the whole meaning of the story that the rich should help the poor. That is, it is turned into a story illustrating a moral. But this particular story . . . is . . . a concrete proclamation of the good news itself. Admittedly so concrete, so powerfully worded, that we don't even take it seriously anymore.

The good news, for Bonhoeffer, is more than a moral to live by; the good news is the present location and work of God in the world. It is the announcement of God's love:

> That was the good news. . . . That was the love of God itself, which spoke in his way to the poor and suffering. You outcasts, you disadvantaged . . . you who are looked down upon. . . . Blessed are you Lazaruses of all ages, you broken down and ruined, you lonely and abandoned . . . those who suffer injustice, you who suffer in body and soul; blessed are you for God's joy will come over you and be over [your] head forever. That is the gospel, the good news.[109]

This good news is distorted by ignoring the external aspects of human existence, turning the gospel into a message about one's attitude toward life; Christians "sublimate" it, moralize it, and spiritualize it.[110] But here is the heart of this sermon from Bonhoeffer in two arguments. First, one insidious outcome of spiritualizing the very concrete gospel makes it an ideology that allows the Christian to "disdain the mass of Lazaruses."[111] The gospel as a moral for living becomes something different than concrete good news for the poor and oppressed; it is no longer about them, but it becomes an endorsement of the life of the socially elite, healthy, wealthy, and strong.

Second, a spiritualized gospel becomes a mockery to placate those in suffering and misery with a hope for a better existence in another world. A spiritualized gospel is what Bonhoeffer read as the opiate religion of white racism that made African Americans meek in the face of their incomparably harsh fate.[112] It was a mockery of their concrete suffering and a theological justification for the oppressed to accept their fate:

> Doesn't it almost sound as if one is just trying to keep these unfortunates from rebelling here against their fate? As if one is calling them blessed just so they will stay quiet, as they are now, and not bother the others? Isn't it downright cynical to talk about consolation in heaven because one does not want to give consolation on earth? Is the gospel for the poor not basically the deception and dumbing down of the people? Does it not show that one does not take the suffering at all seriously but hides cynically behind pious phrases? Oh, countless times it has happened that way—who wouldn't deny it. . . . And millions have become estranged from the gospel for this reason![113]

The pious platitudes that turn the gospel into an opiate for suffering people distort Christianity by not taking suffering seriously as Jesus did, as saving faith and responsible action demands. "Jesus called the poor blessed," Bonhoeffer says, "but he healed them, too." Jesus took suffering seriously by addressing the physical needs of suffering people. On earth now Jesus "takes suffering so seriously that in a moment he must destroy it. Where Christ is, the power of the demons must be broken. That is why he heals, and that is why he says to his disciples: If you believe in me, you will do greater works than I."[114]

Bonhoeffer does not advocate that we perform miracles of healing but that we recognize the concrete nature of the good news. We are all Lazarus, and we have the potential to disregard suffering, as did the rich man. The concreteness of the work of God in Christ demands that we see our suffering brothers and sisters, the full measure of their misery, and, behind them, Christ, who invites them to the table and calls them blessed. Seeing and practicing the gospel in this way is being a Christian in accordance with the good news of God's love.

CONCLUSION

The hermeneutical process that was set in motion by Dietrich Bonhoeffer's formative German nationalist environment had been disrupted by his immersion in a different community. During the Harlem Renaissance and at the beginning of the Great Depression, Bonhoeffer entered the "church of the outcasts of America" in Harlem.[115] He came to Harlem not as the professor come to give oppressed people the benefit of his knowledge; Bonhoeffer allowed himself to be vulnerable in the Harlem community, which was very different from his own German one, by an incarnational practice. In Harlem he learned from Powell's ministry and was exposed to a black dialectical ecclesiology and to Powell's interpretation of a model church community. That encounter exposed the limitations of Bonhoeffer's *Volk*-centered loyalties, making him vulnerable to the influence of a different worldview and opening him up to important revisions in his faith. When Bonhoeffer shared with his friend Myles Horton the interrupting "Amens" and "Hallelujahs" that he experienced in the Abyssinian church service, Myles was

surprised by the different demeanor that his German friend exhibited.[116] It was the different Bonhoeffer, in the year following his
encounter with black Baptists, whose piety sometimes appeared
"too fervent" to his students. One of Bonhoeffer's Berlin students
recalled the directness and "simplicity" with which Bonhoeffer
"asked us whether we loved Jesus."[117] That different Bonhoeffer
was the one who would later speak out against Nazi racism and
become the celebrated author of *Creation and Fall*, *Life Together*,
Discipleship, and *Ethics*.

CHAPTER FIVE

CHRIST-CENTERED EMPATHIC RESISTANCE
Bonhoeffer's Black Jesus in Germany

In Harlem Bonhoeffer learned of a black tradition of Jesus that connected faithfulness to God, the recognition of suffering, and the presence of Christ as cosufferer. The ministries that Bonhoeffer participated in at Abyssinian Baptist Church, coupled with the intellectual interrogation of Jesus within the Harlem Renaissance, provided Bonhoeffer with new resources to filter the nationalism from his Christianity and helped to develop him into an advocate of ecumenism, of peacemaking, and of social justice. As a consequence of that black experience with Jesus, his theology became more than conceptual, his Christology became more prominent, and Bonhoeffer became more serious about his faith.

Bonhoeffer's return from his Sloane Fellowship in the summer of 1931 marks the end of his "academic period," or the years occupied primarily by his role as a student in the academy.[1] As a student in New York, his faith had undergone key developments that enabled him to see extraordinary distortions in German Christianity during a national crisis. Now was the time for him to take up the vocation for which he had been in training. But life now included a personal difference for Bonhoeffer that was not about the move from student to professional; Bonhoeffer would later claim that he had finally become a Christian.[2]

107

GERMANY ON THE BRINK

Bonhoeffer returned to Germany to find his country in escalating economic and political turmoil. The global Great Depression energized the shame and anger that was lingering in Germany in the wake of World War I, but the up-and-coming National Socialist perspective in Germany did not permit the economic disaster to be recognized as a shared global reality. National Socialists were gaining influence in Germany with claims that Germany's financial trouble was evidence of a continued attack by the Allied nations of the Great War. The reparations burden levied by the Treaty of Versailles was evidence that the Allies were intent on leaving Germany mired in poverty.[3]

By the fall of 1931, Bonhoeffer perceived that conditions in in his home country were deteriorating. The depression in Germany intensified the summer of his return when all the banks closed for more than a month following the collapse of the Danatbank, sending unemployment numbers climbing into the millions.[4] The ongoing predicament helped to accelerate the erosion of the Weimar Republic's credibility among its citizens and magnify the political gains of the National Socialist Party. The Weimar attempt at democracy was failing. Bonhoeffer described in an October 1931 letter to Erwin Sutz that the approaching winter appeared very bleak:

> At the present time, I am especially conscious of these things in the public life here in Germany. It really looks unbelievably serious. There apparently is really no one in Germany who has even the slightest overview of things. But in general everyone has a strong feeling that great changes in the course of world history are before us. . . . The coming winter in Germany will probably leave no one unaffected. Seven million unemployed, that means fifteen or twenty million people hungry. I don't know how Germany and how each individual can live through that. . . . We are being pushed at an enormous speed towards a destination that no one knows or could prevent. But will our church survive *another* catastrophe? Will it not reach the end of its existence then, if we do not change immediately, speak and live completely differently? But how? Next Wednesday is a meeting of all the Berlin pastors to discuss the winter problems. . . . I fear bad things from this meeting. . . . But nobody knows anything better to do. And in times like these! What good is a person's theology? . . . The *omina* [omens] are strange.[5]

The problem of what a Christian must do was now paramount for Bonhoeffer, as he was remarkably able to interpret signs of a national crisis on the horizon. Now that his training and traveling were over, he had settled on a perspective that valued theology according to its meaning for daily life. Theology for Bonhoeffer now had to translate into daily, lived obedience to Christ.

BONHOEFFER'S PERSONAL TRANSFORMATION

Bonhoeffer was a young academic professional armed with developments in his faith that became provocative theological convictions as he entered a turbulent environment for his professional life. He was engaging his discipline from a new perspective, after a turn from what Bonhoeffer later described in a letter to a relative as a period of isolation and academic arrogance in his effort to demonstrate his impressive intellectual abilities toward reading the Bible for guidance in a life of following Jesus:

> [Years earlier] I threw myself into my work in an extremely un-Christian and not at all humble fashion. A rather crazy element of ambition, which some people noticed in me, made my life difficult and withdrew from me the love and trust of those around me. At that time, I was terribly alone and left to myself. It was quite bad. But then something different came, something that has changed and transformed my life to this very day. For the first time, I came to the Bible. That, too, is an awful thing to say. I had often preached, I had seen a great deal of the church, had spoken and written about it—and yet I was not yet a Christian but rather in an utterly wild and uncontrolled fashion my own master. I do know that at the time I turned the cause of Jesus Christ into an advantage for myself, for my crazy vanity. . . . Nor had I ever prayed, or had done so only very rarely. Despite this isolation, I was quite happy with myself. The Bible, especially the Sermon on the Mount, freed me from all this. Since then everything has changed. I have felt this plainly and so have other people around me.[6]

Bonhoeffer was different and everyone who knew him could see it. The Sermon on the Mount became relevant commandments for the everyday life of Christians for him, and Bonhoeffer's theology became a passionate articulation of his faith, rather than a demonstration of his intellect, as he explained to his brother Karl Friedrich:

> Perhaps I seem to you rather fanatical and mad about a number of things. . . . But I know that the day I become more "reasonable," to be honest, I should have to chuck my entire theology. When I first started in theology, my idea of it was quite different—rather more academic, probably. Now it has turned into something else altogether. But I do believe that at last I am on the right track, for the first time in my life. . . . I think that I am right in saying that I would only achieve true inner clarity and honesty by really starting to take the Sermon on the Mount seriously.[7]

New devotion to the way of Jesus inspired advocacy for peace and social justice, as he later described to Karl Friedrich: "Things do exist that are worth standing up for without compromise. To me it seems that peace and social justice are such things, as is Christ himself."[8] New York was catalyst for developments in his faith that became seeds of a new Christian identity for him in Germany. Harlem was calling him to a new interpretation of himself as Christian, one that would contradict the blending of national identity and Christianity with Jesus at the center of biblical concreteness and would take years of struggle for him to grasp.

BEGINNING TO STAND ALONE

Bonhoeffer no longer had a goal to demonstrate his brilliance by learning as much as he could as quickly as possible without the guidance of a master teacher. He regretted that earlier self-absorbed practice. With the help of his friend Erwin Sutz, Bonhoeffer spent study time with Karl Barth, who was teaching at the university in Bonn, Germany. While in Bonn, Bonhoeffer attended a three-week seminar with Barth and quickly found himself lonely once more. But this time his isolation was not his choosing and did not carry the sting of arrogance and ambition. In a letter to Sutz dated July 24, 1931, Bonhoeffer sarcastically described Barth's students as the source of his isolation:

> You yourself can imagine that I have often wished you were here . . . especially . . . so that . . . I . . . could have a good laugh (that sounds unlikely, doesn't it?), but I, with my theological bastard origins, have little reason to laugh. . . . Here they have a very finely honed sense for recognizing thoroughbreds. No Negro can pass "for white." His fingernails and the soles of his feet are inspected. I'm still being shown the hospitality of the unknown stranger.[9]

Bonhoeffer was referring to fair-skinned African Americans presenting themselves as white to access the privileges that are not afforded blacks in a white racist society. The notions of pure race and pure theology advance similar goals—social acceptance over social rejection from the guardians of purity who police the borders of identity, examining bodies for evidence of racial, or theological, impurity.

With his fleeting reference to passing, Bonhoeffer identified himself with outcast American Negroes as he was coming into a new theological self-understanding in Germany and identified Barth's condescending theology students with the policemen of white supremacy. The lessons of Harlem were with him in Bonn, and Bonhoeffer would again make use of the opportunity to identify with marginalized people later.[10]

ETHNIC PRIDE AND THE
LUTHERAN CATECHISM

Race logic did not translate exactly between Germany and America. In America, white supremacy manifests itself as the human norm: whites are perceived as normal, nonethnic, nonracial people, and all other people are defined by the logic of race as colored or diverse. In Bonhoeffer's Germany, white supremacy was portrayed as *Volk*ish racial purity. In the language of *die Herrenvolk*, the master race was a German attribution of race to themselves, as they excluded all other people as inferior.[11] The *Volk*ish devotion to pure German blood, with its ethnic, nationalist, imperialist longings, was the German equivalent of normalized humanity from the American version of white supremacy. But racial discrimination was not a conversation that Christians in Germany were accustomed to having. For German Christians, the logic of race and of nation were combined as political content, and for most Germans matters pertaining to Christian life were kept separate from politics. But seeing society from the hidden perspective of Harlem helped Bonhoeffer to recognize white supremacy in Germany and to see it as a Christian problem that might demand Christian political action. Because he was exposed to American racism from the perspective of Christians who were subjected to it, Bonhoeffer was equipped with prophetic insight that his white German colleagues in the church and the academy did not have.

In the summer of his return to Germany and his visit with Barth at Bonn, Bonhoeffer coauthored a Lutheran catechism with his close friend Franz Hildebrandt.[12] The catechism includes a warning about the sin of racist *Volk*ish ideology in Germany: "God has arranged it so that all races of humanity of the earth come from *one* blood (Acts 17:26). Therefore, a defiant ethnic pride in flesh and blood is a sin against the Holy Spirit."[13] The reference to Acts 17:26 in a strong and explicit rebuke of racism is reminiscent of Du Bois' use of the same passage, for the very same purpose, in *Credo*: "I Believe in God who made of one blood all nations."[14] It is the sort of warning that Bonhoeffer will repeat during the church struggle in advocacy of the Jews. Here in the catechism, the sin of racism is just cause for Christians to oppose the state if necessary, in concrete obedience to Christ's commandment to love one's neighbor. He writes, "As much as the Christian would like to remain distant from political struggle, nonetheless, even here the commandment of love urges the Christian to stand up for his neighbor. His faith and love must know whether the dictates of the state may lead him against his conscience."[15] This racial and political perspective from Bonhoeffer at the very beginning of his professional career is significantly at variance with his colleagues in the academy and in the church. The distinctiveness of Bonhoeffer's Christian identity in a turbulent Germany was becoming apparent. His new emphasis on theological concreteness, on ecumenism, on peace and justice indicates that Bonhoeffer was coming into his own very early.[16] At the beginning of his professional career Bonhoeffer was again, as he did during his student years, charting a unique course.

TRANSLATING HARLEM BEFORE THE STORM

Following his time with Barth, Bonhoeffer was ordained on November 15, 1931, and subject to a year of auxiliary service, during which time he remained under the direction of the church authorities for ministry assignments. Also in November, Bonhoeffer took up his position on the faculty at the University of Berlin, Friedrich Wilhelm University, as lecturer (*Privatdozent*) of theology. This made Bonhoeffer an ordained university lecturer, with training for the pastorate and for the academy. Early in 1932 Bonhoeffer purchased a cabin in Biesenthal, Germany, where he took his students on weekend country retreats. Bethge describes the community of students as the "Bonhoeffer circle," who remained loyal to him throughout the entirety of his teaching career.[17] In 1932 Bonhoeffer and his students carried food by train to these retreats, where they talked theology, discussed social settlement work, and listened to Bonhoeffer's collection of Negro spirituals.[18]

In addition to his faculty responsibilities, he was assigned to be chaplain to the students of the technical college in Charlottenburg.[19] He was responsible for informing the campus about his presence at the college and about the programming that he was initiating, which included sermons and topical discussions. But his chaplaincy proved too challenging even for the gifted Bonhoeffer. The response from the students was weak; they were busy and unfamiliar with having a Protestant chaplain. In addition, his chaplaincy, from 1931 to 1933, corresponded with the rising influence of Nazism with students and faculty alike. Fully two-thirds of the student population favored the Nazis, which put them at odds with their new chaplain.[20] Furthermore, Bonhoeffer did not share the theology of his colleagues on the faculty at the University of Berlin and felt isolated among them.[21] Although he was respected by his students, the start of his professional life was turbulent.

THE CONFIRMATION CLASS
IN PRENZLAUER BERG

During the first year of his chaplaincy, while he was completing his auxiliary service, Bonhoeffer was asked to take over responsibility for teaching a confirmation class to a group of boys at Zion Church in the Prenzlauer Berg district of Berlin. That was a poor, working-class district in east Berlin—an area that Bonhoeffer would describe as "proletarian," as he had described blacks in Harlem.[22] He replaced an elderly minister as teacher for the confirmation class; that minister could not manage the raucous group of fifty boys. Indeed, the elderly minister whom Bonhoeffer replaced died several weeks after Bonhoeffer replaced him. In a letter that Bonhoeffer later wrote to Sutz, he claimed that the class "quite literally harassed him to death."[23] But Bonhoeffer was adept at working with boys in youth ministry and knew how to work with the group of "proletarian" youth.[24] Bethge describes Bonhoeffer as professional with them from day one:

> The elderly minister and Bonhoeffer slowly walked up the stairs of the school building, which was several stories high. The children were leaning over the banisters, making an indescribable din and dropping things on the two men ascending the stairs. When they reached the top, the minister tried to force the throng back into the classroom by shouting and using physical force. He tried to announce that he had brought them a new minister who was going to teach them in the future and that his name was Bonhoeffer, and when they heard the name they started shouting "Bon! Bon! Bon!" louder and louder. The old man left the scene in despair, leaving Bonhoeffer standing silently against the wall with his hands in his pockets. Minutes passed. His failure to react made the noise gradually less enjoyable, and he began speaking quietly, so that only the boys in the front row could catch a few words of what he said. Suddenly all were silent. Bonhoeffer merely remarked that they had put up a remarkable initial performance, and went on to tell them a story about Harlem. If they listened, he told them, he would tell them more next time.[25]

Bonhoeffer wrote to Sutz about that first encounter with the confirmation class in Wedding:

> That is about the toughest neighborhood of Berlin, with the most difficult socioeconomic and political conditions. At the beginning the boys were acting wild, so that for the first time I really had discipline problems. But here, too, one thing helped, namely, just simply telling the boys Bible stories in massive quantity, and especially eschatological passages. By the way, in doing this I also made use of the Negroes. Now it is absolutely quiet, and the boys see to that themselves.[26]

Bonhoeffer's reference to eschatological passages from the Bible in conjunction with Negroes may refer to Christian social perspectives within the Harlem community that were invoked by Adam Clayton Powell Sr.'s powerful sermon series on Matthew 25, "A Hungry God" and "A Naked God." In those two impacting sermons that were meant to sensitize the black church community to the suffering of impoverished Harlem blacks in the Great Depression, Powell argued that Christians who are able are obligated to address their physical needs. Powell's reference to Matthew 25 in connection with poor and marginalized Negroes would have resonated with the poor working-class people in Prenzlauer Berg.[27] During his year of auxiliary service, Bonhoeffer was more fulfilled in ministry in Prenzlauer Berg, where he was connecting theology and concrete daily life, than he was teaching theology at the university.[28]

THE YOUTH CLUB IN CHARLOTTENBURG

When the confirmation class in Prenzlauer Berg ended, Bonhoeffer kept relationships among the students, and he continued ministering to Berlin's proletariat. He put together a group for poor youths in Charlottenburg with Anneliese Shnurmann, a Jewish school friend of his younger sister.[29] Their youth group brought his social ministry closer to his chaplaincy at the technical college in Charlottenburg, west Berlin, and brought together numerous groups to participate in their work, including communists and Jews, people who were abhorrent to Nazis.[30] With their collective efforts, the Charlottenburg Youth Club was born in the winter of 1932, "offering job-training courses for young people" as well as housing and food when necessary.[31] Once again, Bonhoeffer was a participant in a ministry to the poor and unemployed.[32]

His work among the poor in Berlin resembled work that Abyssinian Baptist Church was doing in Harlem. Bethge understood Bonhoeffer's work in the Charlottenburg youth club to be principally inspired by his time of study at Union, specifically through exposure to Harry Ward's work in New York.[33] But Ward's class was not Bonhoeffer's only exposure to ministry aimed at helping New York's poor and unemployed. His work at Prenzlauer Berg and in Charlottenburg among the poor and unemployed resembled what Powell Sr. was committed to while Bonhoeffer was in lay leadership at Abyssinian.[34] Bonhoeffer's youth group in Berlin and Abyssinian's community house both offered help to the poor and unemployed with free food, employment assistance, meaningful recreational activities, and education.[35] In Charlottenburg, as in Prenzlauer Berg, Bonhoeffer's ministry was inspired by exposure to Christianity in Harlem. In 1932, before the Nazis began to assemble an overtly racist regime, attention to the plight of the poor, proletariat Germans was the most obvious arena for Bonhoeffer to connect Harlem to Germany.

A BID FOR A PASTORATE IN THE
SLUMS OF BERLIN

In his first few years as a professor, Bonhoeffer was wrestling with his Christian identity in a rapidly changing Germany. He was not certain whether he would continue to combine the roles of professor and pastor or turn solely toward a full-time ministry as a pastor. He was drawn to serve Christ among the marginalized, as his recent history demonstrates. His experiences in Harlem, Prenzlauer Berg, and the youth club led him to continue seeking ministry opportunities in the overcrowded slums of east Berlin, and as a pastor he could continue to serve the church concretely in a manner that was not possible in the classroom.[36] As a professor, Bonhoeffer took advantage of opportunities to engage theological learning outside of the classroom, as he did in Biesenthal. His beyond-the-classroom interaction with his university students put him in contact with the superintendent of a church district in east Berlin. The superintendent was the father of his student Wolf-Dieter Zimmermann, and Bonhoeffer was accustomed to visiting their house often. Bonhoeffer became a candidate for a full-time pastorate in the elder Zimmerman's district at St. Bartholomew's Church. Bonhoeffer thought the choice between the classroom and a pulpit like St. Bartholomew's in the slums of east Berlin was inevitable. In January 1933, he wrote to his brother, Karl-Friedrich, about his impending dilemma:

> At the moment I am faced with a rather momentous decision, whether to undertake a parish ministry, which will probably be offered to me in Friedrichshain, in east Berlin, at Easter. . . . Perhaps the next time you all come to Berlin, you'll be able to come and see me in the parsonage at Friedrichshain, but perhaps not. It's such a dreadful thing not to know what to do.[37]

But the decision to pastor at St. Bartholomew was not only his to make. Bonhoeffer's competition for the job was a man fifteen years his senior who was also superintendent and had an established role as a beloved pastor. Bonhoeffer lost his bid for that pastorate in east Berlin, but he did not immediately abandon his hope of ministry in that poverty-stricken community. Another position opened up in Zimmerman's district, but the times were growing urgent. Nazi racism was becoming the law of the land. The Law for the Re-establishment of the Professional Civil Service with its infamously racist Aryan Clause would soon to be applied to the church and would affect Bonhoeffer through its impact on his Jewish brother-in-law, Gerhard Liebholz, husband of his twin sister, Sabine, and on his Jewish friend Franz Hildebrandt. In particular, the Aryan Clause meant that Hildebrandt, a trained pastor and coauthor of Bonhoeffer's catechism, would no longer be allowed to minister or worship in the German church. As a result, Bonhoeffer grew increasingly frustrated with the response of fellow Christian Protestants to National Socialist racism, and he did not pursue any further pastoral positions in Germany.

THE BLACK CHRIST AND THE
CHRISTOLOGY LECTURES

Bonhoeffer's frustration with the German church helped sharpen his theological focus. Bethge describes the summer of 1933 as turbulent. The Aryan Clause became law, and Bonhoeffer reached the high point of his academic career as he brought together in a set of Christology lectures all of his thoughts, statements, and experiments to prove their foundation and validity.[38] His Christology lectures demonstrate that Jesus is the focus and the center of his theological reasoning. As he lectured, Bonhoeffer made reference to proletarian and bourgeois representations of Jesus. He argued that one might assume that the proletariat would write off Christianity in general because of the bourgeoisie, who have made the Christian church into a shrine to privilege by commingling Jesus with capitalism and domination. But the proletariat does not turn away from Christianity:

> The proletariat actually disassociates Jesus from his church and its religion. When the proletariat says that Jesus is a good human being, it means more than the bourgeoisie means when it says that Jesus is God. Jesus is present in factory halls as a worker among workers, in politics as the perfect idealist, in the life of the proletariat as a good human being. He stands beside members of the proletariat as a fighter in their ranks against the capitalist enemy.[39]

The bourgeois Jesus is an oppressor's Jesus, who is removed from his historical context, which would be a truer representation of him, and embedded as theological support within the social ideologies that practice domination. The Jesus-plus-power mixture is lethal for the oppressed and the oppressor alike. It disallows

Christianity any access to guidance from the life of Christ and reinforces ideologies that maintain the inferiority of proletariat humanity. But the recovered Jesus disassociated from oppressive structures, as Bonhoeffer describes in his Christology lectures, is present in the African American tradition of Jesus that stimulated Bonhoeffer's service to Germany's proletariat neighborhoods. The audience can hear it in the Negro spirituals and gospel music of Bonhoeffer's great fondness. The musical forms recover Jesus from representations that associate Christ with domination. Jacquelyn Grant argues that gospel songs echo this black experience of Jesus "out-of-the-box," naming him as a shelter from the storm, a doctor in the sick room, a lawyer in the courtroom.[40] In the face of the white racist assault on the African American family system since slavery and Reconstruction, Jesus, embodied in the oppressed community, has been family—a father to the fatherless, mother to the motherless, sister to the sisterless, brother to the brotherless, and friend to the friendless. Intimately acquainted with this African American encounter with Jesus, Bonhoeffer was inspired by the experience and the result of his presence among the faith community. This African American tradition of Jesus was different from his experience of the proletarian community that he met elsewhere; African American proletarian communities experienced a tradition of Jesus that was developed in the context of a daily practice of deflecting white-supremacist ideologies crafted to distort black humanity. The black Jesus is a tradition of Christ-the-center that is present in the daily life and experiences of black people.[41] In that lived model, Bonhoeffer found a viable pattern for Christian living in a hostile world.

FRUSTRATED AND ALONE: THE END OF HIS TIME IN BERLIN

Instead of deciding between a professional life in service to the church or to the academy in Berlin, in October of 1933 Bonhoeffer chose to leave Germany and become a pastor of two expatriate German congregations in London. He took a temporary leave of absence from the faculty at the University of Berlin and explained his reasons for leaving Germany to Karl Barth after he arrived in London, when it was too late for Barth to influence his decision to go:

> I knew that I could not accept the pastorate for which I had been longing, particularly in that part of the city, if I was unwilling to give up my unconditional opposition to this church. It would have meant the loss of credibility before the congregation from the outset. It would have meant abandoning my solidarity with the Jewish Christian pastors—my closest friend [Hildebrandt] is one of them and is currently without a future. . . . So the alternatives were lecturer or pastor, and in any case, not as pastor in the Prussian church.[42]

When he returned to the University of Berlin in the winter of 1935, he combined his role as lecturer on the faculty with a new subversive role as director of the Confessing Church seminary at Finkenwalde. But this arrangement did not last long. Finkenwalde was an illegal seminary—Bonhoeffer was openly training pastors involved in the Confessing Church movement that opposed the Nazification of the German state church. Bonhoeffer's leadership as one of the founding pastors of the Confessing Church movement put him at odds with the administration of the University in Berlin and the German state church. His right to teach in Berlin was revoked in August 1936 as a result. He had unknowingly delivered his final lecture on February 14, 1936.[43] Hence, the real choice for a professional life that Germany presented to him was that of lecturer on a faculty whose theology he saw as heretical or as trainer of authentic Christian pastors at a different school.

For all practical purposes his leave of absence in 1933 was the beginning of the end of his professional academic career at the University in Berlin. His extracurricular work in ministry while teaching in 1932–1933 was not done in the heat of the church struggle. That changed in 1935–1936. His strained relationships with state church authorities put him under the watchful eye of the university administration and started the clock toward his termination. Thus, his active teaching career was drawing to a close in the summer of his Christology lectures, with him deeply frustrated and, yet again, alone.

THE GERMAN CHRISTIAN EFFORTS
AT SYNCHRONIZATION

A critical time in Germany, its politics, its social life, and its Protestant churches developed in 1933. Patriotism, religion, and social ideals were being integrated in the churches into a distorted mess of Germanism through concepts like orders of creation.

The notion of orders was a traditional Lutheran concept that functioned similarly to natural law in Catholic ethics as a way of engaging social ethics without appeal to special revelation in Christ.[44] Conservative German Lutheran theologians relied on orders of creation language in their opposition to human rights and the democracy of the Weimar Republic and to support Hitler as leader of the nation and the church.

Advocacy for Hitler as leader of the Protestant Church in Germany became the German Christians movement, which was mobilized by National Socialist Christians who favored the Nazification of the church by bringing all German Protestants together under the Führer principle, making Hitler the head of the church as well as the government.[45] The German Christian movement was a *Volk*ish Christian movement, mobilized by a theological worldview that was the German equivalent of American white supremacy: "The National Socialist Philosophy fights relentlessly against the political and intellectual influence of the Jewish race on the life of our *Volk*. In obedience to the divine order of creation, the Evangelical Church affirms its responsibility to preserve the purity of our *Volk*dom."[46] Orders of creation combined a *Volk*-centered worldview with the concept of blood and soil to support the mounting zealotry surrounding the Führer concept[47] within German Christian loyalties:

> The source and confirmation of our faith are God's Revelation in the Bible and the witness borne to the faith by the Fathers. . . . As with every people, the eternal God also created a Law for our people especially suited to its racial character. It acquired form in the Führer Adolf Hitler and in the National Socialist state, which he formed. This Law speaks to us in the history of our people, born of our blood and soil. Loyalty to this Law demands from us the struggle for honor and freedom.[48]

The theology of the German Christian movement turned Jesus into a divine representation of the ideal, racially pure Aryan and turned race-hate into an element of religious worship.

STANDING ALONE IN A CROWD: BONHOEFFER AND THE EMERGING OPPOSITION

The majority of Protestants in Germany chose to remain neutral in the face of an impending church crisis. They chose neither to oppose nor to support the pro-Nazi German Christian movement.[49] The German Christians sought to synchronize the Protestant church in Germany with the government under the Führer principle. Most of those who joined the resistance against the German Christian synchronization movement did so primarily out of loyalty to the Lutheran tradition of the two kingdoms.[50] They resisted the German Christians for different reasons than Bonhoeffer did, seeking to accomplish different outcomes.

Bonhoeffer was involved very early in Christian opposition to the German Christians along with Martin Niemöller, a former German naval officer.[51] Bonhoeffer and Niemöller inspired support from a larger group of Protestant pastors who opposed the German Christians to form an initial Young Reformers movement[52] with further evolutions; the Young Reformation movement later became the Pastors' Emergency League on its way to becoming the Confessing Church movement.[53] Along the way, neither of these groups was radical enough for Bonhoeffer in its opposition to the German Christians. The group of pastors that made up the Young Reformation movement sought to distinguish their genuine faith from that of the German Christians by way of the Bethel Confession,[54] coauthored by Bonhoeffer, George Merz, and Herman Sasse.[55] But twenty other resisting pastors were involved in editing the confession, and Bonhoeffer's effort to rebuke Nazi racism by including a section on the Jewish question was edited out of the final version. The pastors intended to formulate a statement of pure Christian doctrine that would filter the German Christians out of the church by making their non-Christian intentions apparent. But they did not see racial oppression as a problem for Christians to address, and that omission so deeply disturbed Bonhoeffer that he refused to sign it. He was, figuratively, standing alone in a crowd.[56] He wrote about the experience in a letter to Sutz while the confessional statement was being edited:

> We are about to witness a great reorganization of the churches, which, to all appearances, will not be a bad thing. It is to be hoped that it will bring about the automatic withdrawal of the German Christians . . . and so . . . we shall once again rescue the church. The Jewish question is also giving the church a great deal of trouble, and here the most intelligent people have totally lost both their heads and their Bibles.[57]

The degree to which they had "lost both their heads and their Bibles" becomes even clearer when understanding what they wanted in their opposition to the German Christians. The majority of Bonhoeffer's fellow resisting pastors were at odds with the Führer principle in the church but not against Hitler's government:

> The Young Reformation declared: We say yes to the new government under Adolf Hitler, but no to the German Christians. The Church must remain the Church, and the state may not be allowed to interfere in its affairs. The only sources for the concerns of the Church are the Bible and the confessional writings of the Reformation. The German Christians attempt to change that is unacceptable. The Young Reformation was saying No specifically to the German Christians, not to the government; on the contrary, it was second to no one in its political loyalty.[58]

The attitude of most of the opposition to the German Christians was consistent with their interpretation of Luther's doctrine of the two kingdoms; they understood political and ecclesiological matters to be separate and unrelated within the life of the church. The majority of those who rejected the Aryan Clause did so because it constituted a confusion of authority between the two kingdoms: "We confess our faith in the Holy Spirit, and therefore reject, as a matter of principle, the exclusion of non-Aryans from the church, because it is based on the confusion between state and church. The state is supposed to judge; the church is supposed to save."[59] The Bethel Confession served as an early indication of the vast difference between Bonhoeffer's interpretation of Christian identity and the myopic theological scope of his colleagues.

THE RESULTS OF HARLEM IN GERMANY: BONHOEFFER'S PROPHETIC THEOLOGICAL INSIGHT

Bonhoeffer opposed the synchronization of the church and state under the Führer principle for at least three reasons that differed radically from those of his colleagues: his understanding of the connection between ecclesiology and discipleship, his understanding of Jesus as *Stellvertretung* (vicarious representative action), and his developed understanding of Luther's theology of the cross.

First, Bonhoeffer understood church synchronization with Hitler's government to mean much more than the disruption of the traditional separation between church and state; it meant a fundamental distortion of the church and the nature of Christian discipleship. The church is a Christ-centered community; for Bonhoeffer it is Christ existing as church community.[60] The type of fellowship that Christians have with their neighbor, especially a suffering, oppressed neighbor, betrays the authenticity of Christian discipleship. The Aryan Clause was state-mandated injustice that specifically targeted Jews and made hatred of Jews an obligatory proof of German patriotism. When the German Christians moved to adopt the Aryan Clause as law within the German state church, Bonhoeffer reasoned that their move presented a crisis for the church because the Christian community is fundamentally compromised by apathy toward, or participation with, racial injustice:

> The exclusion of Jewish Christians from our communion of worship would mean: The excluding church is erecting a racial law as a prerequisite of Christian communion. But in doing so it loses Christ himself. . . . A Christian church cannot exclude from its communion a member on whom the sacrament of baptism has been bestowed, without degrading baptism. . . . With exclusion of the Jewish Christians from the communion of worship, he who realizes the nature of the church must feel himself to be excluded also.[61]

As a result of his time in Harlem, the twenty-seven-year-old Bonhoeffer was clear from the beginning of the Nazi threat that the mixture of race, nationalism, and religion was lethal. Most of his much-older colleagues within the church resistance movement could not share his insight.[62] Bonhoeffer reasoned that state racism is an error egregious enough to invalidate the legitimacy of a government and to compel the church to speak in opposition. In his prophetic essay "The Church and the Jewish Question," written at the beginning of the church struggle in 1933, Bonhoeffer *radicalized* the Jewish question for the church in a Christian environment where the majority did not even recognize the Jewish question as a problem. Consistent with the claim that he made in the catechism coauthored with Hildebrandt in the summer of 1931, Bonhoeffer described the current crisis in politics as one that required Christians "who would like to remain distant from political struggle to respond faithfully to the commandment of love" and to stand up for suffering neighbors.

In fidelity to the Lutheran understanding of separation of church and state, he was careful to describe the legitimate God-given authority of a state to pass and to enforce laws as well as the separate God-given role of the church for society. Bonhoeffer reasoned that the church cannot directly oppose the state even in regard to the Jewish question. But consistent with his theology that sees church and discipleship merged, Bonhoeffer listed three possible approaches that the faithful church must consider taking in the current emergency. First, the church can hold this state publicly accountable by questioning the injustice of its behavior toward its Jewish citizens. The Aryan Clause was evidence that this state had simultaneously deteriorated into lawlessness, with a law tailored to remove the rights of a specific people, and fallen into despotism, by interfering with the church and the proclamation of its message. The boundary-crossing demands of the Nazi state, with its mandatory racial injustice, amount to a *status confessionis*, a defining moment, for the church, when its very essence is in question.[63] Second, the church could attend to the victims of the unlawful government, the Jews, because "the church has an unconditional obligation toward the victims of any societal order, even if they do not belong to the Christian Community."[64] Bonhoeffer's understanding of Christian discipleship is based on the obedient church's confession of faith in Christ, and as such it is an ethic "for others," which indicates that Bonhoeffer's advocacy for the Jews extends beyond his concern for non-Aryan Christians to include non-Christian Jews.[65] Last, the church may take drastic action in the face of the lawless state by doing more than attending to the state's victims, figuratively throwing itself into the spokes of the wheel of state. That is, the current crisis may call for the church to take direct political action and declare the illegitimacy of this regime that has become a state of injustice.[66] Bonhoeffer's radical suggestions result from his belief in obedience as concrete theological engagement with the world. The nature of the obedient church is faithfulness to Christ on behalf of others in the moment of crisis. Like Adam Clayton Powell's description of saving faith, Bonhoeffer reasoned that the gospel demands concrete obedience. But his colleagues in the church resistance met Bonhoeffer's 1933 essay on the Jewish question with silence, which helped motivate him to leave Germany and pastor in London. A year later in a letter to Erwin Sutz, Bonhoeffer asserted that the least that the faithful church should do is to care for the vulnerable: " 'Speak out for those who cannot speak out.' Who in the church still remembers that this is the very least the Bible asks of us in such times as these?"[67]

His interpretation of Jesus is the second radical difference from his confessing church colleagues. Jesus is for Bonhoeffer *Stellvertretung.* As the vicarious representative for humanity, Jesus is both the source and the guide for Christian community and the mandate for empathic social interaction with those who suffer. The way of Christ interpreted by Bonhoeffer as *Stellvertretung* is the location for the theology that guides his social reasoning and the source from which Bonhoeffer derives his empathic Christ-centered ethics since his first dissertation. For Bonhoeffer, Christ as *Stellvertretung* is the revelation of God and the demonstration of God's freedom for humanity.[68] Christ as the new humanity, as being-free-for-humanity, is developed further in Bonhoeffer's Christology lectures in the summer of 1933. He described Christ as the one who is *pro nobis,* "for us," not in a sentimental way but ontologically as the person of Christ; Jesus cannot be understood in his being by himself, but only in relationship, in community.[69] *Pro nobis* describes the being and the work of Christ in the development of God's kingdom.[70] In his actions and his being, he is humanity for us before God:

> He is there for his brothers and sisters in that he stands in their stead. Christ stands for his new humanity before God, that is, he takes their place and stands in their stead before God. If this is so, then he is the new humanity. There where the new humanity should stand, he himself stands. . . . That means he is the church-community. He is no longer acting for it, on its behalf, but rather as it, in his going to the cross, dying, and taking the sins of the church-community upon himself.[71]

The implications of Christ as *pro nobis* for Bonhoeffer become clearer in *Discipleship,* at the height of the church struggle. In *Discipleship,* Christ *pro nobis* provides concrete guidance for his disciples, who are the body of Christ in the world:

> Suffering is distance from God. . . . [Jesus] takes the suffering of the whole world onto himself and overcomes it. He bears the whole distance from God. . . . Suffering must be borne in order for it to pass. Either the world must bear it and be crushed by it, or it falls on Christ and is overcome in him. That is how Christ suffers as vicarious representative [*Stellvertretung*] for the world. . . . But the church-community itself knows that the world's suffering seeks a bearer. So in following Christ, this suffering falls upon it, and it bears the suffering while being borne by Christ. The community of Jesus Christ

vicariously represents the world before God by following Christ under the cross.[72]

Christ *pro nobis* takes on ethical implications as *Stellvertretung* becomes an imperative for Christian moral living in solidarity with suffering Jews. Concretely this means that Christians act on their Jewish neighbors' needs for justice and value them as they value their own. Bonhoeffer's incarnational ethics model describes Christ as humanity free from bondage to a self-love that would inhibit ability to know and value a neighbor's needs as one's own. Being-free-for-others allows Christian disciples to "do to others whatever you would like them to do to you."[73]

His final work, *Ethics*, describes the empathic nature of *Stellvertretung* with further incarnational emphasis. Engaging life concretely is important to Bonhoeffer because it guards against the harmful effects of abstract notions of right and good that define what is good before accounting for its impact on the lives of real people:

> In this approach, the ethical task is seen as applying specific principles, regardless of how they are related to life. This results in two possible alternatives. The first defines what is good exclusively as one's own adherence to principles without any regard for the other person, and thus leads to a complete privatization of life. . . . In the second alternative, the abstract understanding of the ethical leads to religious enthusiasm.[74]

The reference to "religious enthusiasm" is a historic Lutheran denigration of Anabaptists and of Christian prohibition advocates Bonhoeffer encountered in America.[75] Both were representatives of the practice of abstract theological and moral reasoning. Reasoning in the abstract is a moral practice that is subject to the problem of privilege that Bonhoeffer criticized in the fellowship of his colleagues in the church resistance; it traps one's moral reasoning within a feigned universal objectivity while remaining narrow-minded. Abstract moral reasoning is especially pernicious toward historically marginalized people, who are typically rendered invisible in the process. Universal reasoning boasts of a "one-size-fits-all" morality that is at best undetected egoism and at worst intentional domination that pushes the minority to the margins and disregards their experience of domination by the

community in its dreaming of an ideal society. It is an ethical failure in disguise:

> Here no genuine encounter with life, with actual people, has taken
> place. Indeed, in this kind of failure, something alien, inauthentic,
> contrived, fictitious, and at the same time highly tyrannical is cast off
> [let loose on society] without human beings themselves, in the core
> of their being, really having been touched, transformed, and forced
> to make a decision.[76]

Bonhoeffer describes this tyrannical cast off as a "failure to
engage."[77] Practicing one's moral reasoning in the abstract reduces
daily life to adiaphora, things indifferent or unimportant, by comparison to theory. Christian moral reasoning becomes a quantifi-
able progression of the natural order that can be grasped rationally
and mastered solely by reason; life becomes a theoretical idea. The
concept of orders of creation was this sort of idea: white supremacy worked according to racial ideas; Nazi Christianity was mobilized according to visionary dreams of idealized Aryan-German
life that were imposed upon society by violence.

For Bonhoeffer, life is not an idea, a thing, an essence, or a
concept. Life is a person; Christ is life. He is life, not as a concept
or as one who has life, but life itself. Jesus says, "I am the life."[78]
Life cannot be separated from this I. If Jesus is life, then life comes
to people from outside of themselves and is beyond human cogni-
tive capabilities. Jesus comes to people as life and contradicts good
as a human construct by which people live apart from him in the
most moral definitions, whether American or German. What is
called good apart from Jesus is revealed as fallen life and rebellion
against the origin, essence, and goal of life.[79] It is ego at work.

Bonhoeffer claims that meeting Jesus is an encounter with a
moment of decision; it is a moment for a divine no and yes. With
Jesus one hears no to judgment and death, which is existence in
rebellion and isolation from God. Simultaneously, Jesus offers yes
to reconciliation with God, with humanity, and to decision. The
meeting demands a decision to say no to ego and yes to Christ who
is life, yes to participation in the reconciliation with the world that
God has achieved in the incarnation of Christ.

Christ the *Stellvertretung* stands in for humanity such that it
is no longer possible to know humanity without knowing Jesus

who is life. Christ is human for all of humanity, and Christ is also God. There is no knowing God or humankind without knowing Jesus, and there is no knowing Jesus without knowing humankind and God. Jesus who is God and humanity comes to all people in all encounters that are had with others as God's *Stellvertretung*. Additionally because Christ stands in for all of humanity, human social interaction is marked by social interaction with the *Stellvertretung* in all human encounters. Bonhoeffer writes, "So there is no relation to other human beings without a relation to God, and vice versa. . . . The relation to Jesus Christ is the basis for our relation to other human beings and to God."[80] He explains that, in those encounters, we remain subject to the contradictory unity of yes and no and bound by the claim on our life that comes to us from outside ourselves, committing us to self-assertion that is a surrender of self to God and to other human beings.[81] That is why Bonhoeffer writes from prison, "The church is the church only when it is there for others."[82] Hence, there is no disregarding the injustice that the Jewish neighbor experiences that does not include disregarding the suffering of Christ and being in bondage to isolation from him.

Finally, privileges that guard some Christians from experiencing oppression may also keep them from seeing oppression or suffering as matters within the scope of Christian moral responsibility. Martin Luther contrasted *theologia crucis* with *theologia gloriae* in his Heidelberg Disputation, 1518, to argue that the revelation of God occurs not in the glory of human aptitudes for all to see but in hiddenness, through suffering and shame.[83] The theologian of glory claims to grasp theological theories as full and complete accounts of reality, leaving no room for doubt or debate.[84] The result of a theology of glory is a far too confident Christian, too confident about theological responses to complex questions of life that have not been engaged faithfully and that often shape Christians whose lives look no different from those of the rest of society. Before his Sloane Fellowship Bonhoeffer interpreted the *theologia crucis / theologia gloriae* distinction to mean that Christianity does not guide us to behave in a particularly Christian way. *Theologia gloriae* made religious moral claims, but for the early Bonhoeffer "the Christian message is basically amoral and irreligious, paradoxical as that may sound."[85] To drive home his point about *theologia gloriae*, Bonhoeffer insisted that "Christianity and ethics have absolutely nothing to do with each other. There is no Christian ethic. From the idea of Christianity, there is absolutely no transition to the idea of ethics."[86] Implicit in Bonhoeffer's earlier argument was the claim that trying to follow the Gospels as though they provided concrete commandments results in *theologia gloriae*, or religious hubris.

Bonhoeffer's theology after New York included developments in his understanding of the *theologia crucis* in regard to the social role the church must take in response to oppression. *Theologia crucis* came to be defined as theology done from the recognition of God's hiddenness in suffering with the outcast and the marginalized—as Bonhoeffer had experienced God in the hidden African American communities and now among the suffering Jews. During the church struggle in Germany, he criticized his prior misinterpretation of *theologia crucis* as social conformity rather than Christian obedience:

> It may be also—and that is even more dangerous—a so-called reformation theology, which even dares to call itself *theologia crucis* and whose signature is that it prefers a "humble" invisibility in the form of total conformity to the world over a "Pharisaic" visibility [*theologia gloriae*]. . . . Here the criterion for Christianity is considered to be that the light should *not* shine. But Jesus says, "Let your light shine before the Gentiles." . . . What do the invisibility and hiddenness of Jesus' cross under which the disciples stand have in common with the light which is to shine? Shouldn't it follow from the hiddenness of the cross that the disciples should likewise be hidden, and not stand in the light? It is an evil sophistry which uses the cross of Jesus to derive from it the church's call to conformation to the world. . . . Is it not visibility enough that Christ is rejected and must suffer, that his life ends outside the city gates on a hill of shame? Is that invisibility?[87]

Christ's identification with suffering becomes the hiddenness of God's glory, and among the marginalized we experience the presence and power of God to redeem. In this context, we find concrete guidance from Christ:

> The good works of the disciples should be seen in this light. . . . What are these good works which can be seen in this light? They can be no other works than those Jesus himself created in the disciples when he called them, when he made them the light of the world under his cross—poverty, being strangers, meekness, peace-making, and

finally being persecuted and rejected, and in all of them one work: bearing the cross of Jesus Christ.[88]

Bonhoeffer continues in *Discipleship* to describe the reconciliation of God and creation in the person of Christ, with the way of Jesus described as concrete guiding substance from the Sermon on the Mount for daily living. Obedience to the commandments requires taking up one's cross in solidarity with suffering people.

In light of his developed *theologia crucis*, Bonhoeffer highlights the privilege that his colleagues had in order to ignore suffering and racial oppression as he confronted them for their inattention to the plight of the Jews in the struggle against the German Christians:

> The German Christians' demands destroy the substance of the ministry by making certain members of the Christian community into members with lesser rights, second-class Christians. The rest, those who remain privileged members, should prefer to stand by those with lesser rights rather than to benefit from a privileged status in the church. They must see their own true service, which they can still perform for their church, in resigning from this *office of pastor as a privilege*, which is now what it has become.[89]

Bethge explains that this reference to pastoral privilege was a characteristic argument that Bonhoeffer made about "fatal privilege."[90] It was fatal because it prohibited Christians from seeing that their pastoral privileges rested on a deeper set of insidious privileges, namely ethnic pride and Aryan privilege. Bonhoeffer wanted his colleagues to see that they were doing their theological reasoning from a set of privileges that were detrimental to Christian discipleship. Their theological response to suffering was far too simple; it amounted to *theologia gloriae* as a response to complex matters that left the most salient issues without faithful engagement. Bethge points out that Niemöller, like most other resisting pastors, would much rather have viewed the Jewish question as adiaphora and not a church issue.[91] But saving faith requires biblical concreteness in response to Christ who is hidden in suffering.

Bonhoeffer identifies the Jews with the marginalized and oppressed, even the marginalized African Americans that he came to know in New York. The Aryan pastors were reasoning from within a context of social privilege with regard to the

Aryan Clause, and Bonhoeffer brought attention to the negative impact of unexamined social location on their theological reasoning. On at least two occasions during meetings with resisting pastors, Bonhoeffer was reported to have stood and quoted these few words from the nineteenth-century German poet Theodor Storm and returned to his seat:

> One man asks: What is to come?
> The other: What is right?
> And that is the difference
> Between the free man and the slave.[92]

By reference to this couplet in the context of the church struggle, Bonhoeffer connected the Jewish question and the American Negro problem, highlighting the impact of social perspective on moral reasoning. The Aryan Clause was a *status confessionis* for the church, and faithful Christians had to be made aware of the "the difference between the free man and the slave" to recognize oppression as evil and to serve Christ in the lives of suffering and marginalized people.

A PROPHET'S BURDEN

There were pastors among Bonhoeffer's colleagues who did agree with Bonhoeffer's perspectives about the Jews and the Aryan Clause as a problem for the church. But they did not share Bonhoeffer's level of concern about it. His argument that synchronization, with its racial conformity mandate, was a *status confessionis* was not shared within the Confessing Church movement. His argument was so unique that Bonhoeffer himself thought that he was the problem. Not even his friend and theological mentor Karl Barth shared his radical perspective on racial conformity. Bonhoeffer was puzzled by the isolation caused by his radical convictions:

> I felt that, in some way I don't understand, I found myself in radical opposition to all my friends; I was becoming increasingly isolated with my views of the matter, even though I was and remain personally close to these people. All of this frightened me and shook my confidence, so that I began to fear that dogmatism might be leading me astray—since there seemed no particular reason why my own view on these matters should be any better, any more right, than the views of many really able pastors whom I sincerely respect.[93]

The radical convictions that Bonhoeffer displayed during the church struggle were not the product of his German theological and ecclesiological environment; they were imported goods. His entry into the social context of African Americans in Harlem was the reversal of a theological hermeneutic that typically flowed from Germany to the United States. In Bonhoeffer's case, the flow of essential theological content moved across the Atlantic from Harlem to Germany. Upon his return to Germany, he entered the context of the poor and the outcast in the slums of Berlin with the tradition of Jesus he encountered in Harlem, even moving into a poor east Berlin neighborhood as a renter and seeking to make his time there permanent as a pastor within their community. And in the church struggle he entered into the context of those marginalized by the Nazi government, seeking to make his companions aware of the view of the oppressive German society from the perspective of those suffering and marginalized within it. Bonhoeffer's advocacy for direct political action by the church was highly uncommon, especially for a German Lutheran. But Bonhoeffer reasoned that suffering must be borne for it to pass and Christ bears his own in the practice of vicarious representative action bearing neighbors' burdens.[94] That is Christian discipleship, and it is a Christ-inspired motivation for justice.

PREACHING IN THE CLOUD OF WITNESSES AT ABYSSINIAN

Bonhoeffer was an ally of the resisting pastors, despite his differences with them, and was an important and politically vocal member of the Confessing Church movement. In 1939 he made a short return to New York to avoid being drafted into the German Army at the beginning of World War II. His friend Paul Lehmann helped to arrange that trip, which included a job offer to teach at Union. The Americans at Union intended the job to be a permanent appointment, but for Bonhoeffer the thought of staying for even one year was a significant strain on his conscience.

Shortly after he arrived in New York on his second trip, he found himself desperately homesick and wracked with doubts over his decision to leave his seminary students, whom he continued to mentor, as well as his colleagues in the Confessing Church. During his homesickness, Bonhoeffer returned to Abyssinian

Baptist Church in Harlem and, this time, he delivered a sermon. Ruth Zerner describes Bonhoeffer's enthusiastic retelling of his sermon experience in a black Harlem church. His interlocutor was Rudolph Schade, who worked in the library at Union:

> [For] Rudolf Schade, the most vivid memory of his conversations with Bonhoeffer goes back to a Monday in the Union Seminary library following Bonhoeffer's Sunday sermon in a black Harlem congregation, most likely the Abyssinian Baptist Church. Beaming and enthusiastic, Bonhoeffer invited Schade to walk with him on Riverside Drive, so that he could share the previous day's experience with him. Talking intensely in German to Schade, Bonhoeffer conveyed the thrill and joy of having had members of the black congregation respond to his message. They expressed their support and agreement with his points by punctuating his sermon with "Amens" and "Hallelujahs." For Bonhoeffer the episode had obviously been positive and exhilarating.[95]

Until recently, it was assumed that this preaching experience in a black Harlem church occurred during Bonhoeffer's Sloane Fellowship year, 1930–1931. But leading Bonhoeffer scholars note that Schade was not at Union during that school year; his time at Union only corresponds with Bonhoeffer's second trip. Thus, Bonhoeffer's sermon at Abyssinian occurred when he was vexed over his decision to return to New York and racked with homesickness: "it was during those anxious weeks when he knew that he was in the wrong place that he turned once again to the spiritual support of the 'cloud of witnesses.' " Just two years prior to his return to Abyssinian, Adam Clayton Powell Sr. retired from his pastorate, and his son Adam Clayton Powell Jr. was installed as his father's replacement as senior pastor. Hence, in 1939 Bonhoeffer preached in the church of his former short-term classmate at Union. The congregation's enthusiastic response to Bonhoeffer indicates the level at which he had come to empathize with the African American Christian perspective. They were not affirming an imperialist, bourgeois, or Aryan representation of the white Jesus; the black call-and-response that he experienced from the congregation as he preached was an affirmation of the truth they knew from life experience. At Abyssinian Baptist in Harlem, they knew the Jesus Bonhoeffer preached.

His decision to identify with outcasts and the marginalized in America and Germany made him one of the outcasts in the eyes of the Nazi government. And it was a perspective that he valued. In 1942, just prior to his arrest by the Gestapo, he articulated his gratitude for this perspective as "a view from below" in his well-known piece "After Ten Years":

> It remains an experience of incomparable value that we have for once learned to see the great events of world history from below, from the perspective of the outcasts, the suspects, the maltreated, the power-less, the oppressed, and the reviled, in short from the perspective of the suffering . . . that we come to see matters great and small, happiness and misfortune, strength and weakness with new eyes; that our sense for greatness, humanness, justice, and mercy has grown clearer, freer, more incorruptible; that we learn, indeed, that personal suffering is a more useful key, a more fruitful principle than personal happiness for exploring the meaning of the world in contemplation and action.[96]

Seeing from below is seeing from the rather hidden perspective, and it is more fruitful than happiness as a key to understanding the role of the church in society and the shape of Christian life. Access to the perspective from below clarifies the quality of Christian discipleship by revealing that a supposed moral life is not the key to a good Christian life; Christlikeness is. People may be labeled as essentially immoral by racialized definitions of humanity, and a moral life may be determined by adherence to doctrines in isolation from others or doctrines that favor an idealized community. But Christlikeness is determined in concrete daily interaction with and for others. One cannot claim to know Christ and ignore injustice. As Bonhoeffer indicates, Christ is hidden in suffering and marginalization. To see the world from the perspective of those communities where outcasts are labeled and shunted grants vision of the nature of God in Christ. To volunteer as one who shares the load of suffering and marginalization creates participation in what God is doing in the world, and, thus, the burden-bearer becomes a disciple of Christ.

Bonhoeffer was a unique and brilliant Christian in the context of a very dark time in American history that was revealed to him through his contacts with the Harlem Renaissance and his experiences at the Abyssinian Baptist Church. When he returned from New York in the summer of 1931, there was a clear transformation in the way that he saw his theological contribution impacting the world. It became a concrete contribution to Christian social interaction—not only an academic contribution but one that engaged Christians in their daily lives, placing the entirety of life under the gospel. He began to translate those convictions by including field trips and social ministry opportunities for his students. In those times away from the classroom, Bonhoeffer played Negro spirituals for his students and introduced them to the piety of African American religion. He did the same for his students at Finkenwalde. He was intentional about ministry to the poor and outcast in Berlin, in a manner that resembled his work in Harlem during the Great Depression that was so devastating to the already marginalized African American migrant community in Harlem. But when the Aryan Clause made its first mark on the German Evangelical church, Bonhoeffer found another direct correlation between the African American community that so impacted him personally and his native German society. That connection enabled him to see much sooner than his colleagues did the dangers of Nazi racism. By the time his colleagues finally recognized these dangers, the Nazi hatred and war-making government had become a juggernaut of murder and destruction. The transformation that Bonhoeffer experienced in Harlem, in addition to the crisis of Christian identity in the midst of the Confessing Church movement, became for Bonhoeffer a struggle to disentangle the coupling of Christianity with national identity. For Bonhoeffer, that struggle lasted the rest of his life.

CONCLUSION

The Nazi SS killed Bonhoeffer on April 9, 1945, at Flossenbürg concentration camp two weeks before the U.S. Army liberated it. Flossenbürg was the last of four prisons that retained him during his two years of incarceration as an enemy of the state. After he returned from his Sloane Fellowship to begin his professional life, he lived another fourteen years, reaching the end of his life at age thirty-nine in a tragic way, without seeing the benefits of his passionate struggle. In the end, he gave his last full measure of devotion to Christ in solidarity with outcasts during one of the most dark and violent times in world history, having lived only to see conditions reach their worst. Today, there are some who view him primarily as a controversial figure. As a young pastor devoted to the Sermon on the Mount and to pacifism, he is believed to have been a member of a resistance movement against Hitler. The juggernaut of war making and murder that the Nazis became was aided by the compliance and apathy of common citizens who saw Nazi cruelty and did nothing. Only later, when conditions had reached catastrophic proportions, were some citizens provoked enough to enact a number of unsuccessful coup attempts. But Bonhoeffer saw Nazis as malevolent from the beginning, and he strongly and publicly articulated his disagreement in accordance with his clear description of Christian faithfulness.

Puzzling paradoxes form a part of Bonhoeffer's legacy: he likely participated in a coup attempt against Hitler; radical and enigmatic to his colleagues, he gave up a bright future in the academy to struggle for the witness of the church against corrupting Nazi racism; as a blue-eyed, blond, wealthy, educated, prototypical Aryan German man, he chose solidarity with racial outcasts in America and Germany rather than a life of comfort within a society structured specifically to secure him privileges. His decisions to follow his convictions cost him his life. Family and friends had difficulty understanding what was driving Bonhoeffer's ostensibly insane behavior, but he was compelled into these seeming contradictions by his pursuit of meaningful Christian discipleship in a trying time by the call that Harlem's black Christ placed upon his emerging Christian identity as a young religion scholar. He chose to rely on the grace of God in active solidarity with suffering outcasts.

Many decades after his murder, Bonhoeffer's voice remains relevant and influential. Considering the struggle he endured to be taken seriously by colleagues within the Confessing Church movement, his work—rather than that of many of his contemporaries—has been most influential and remains relevant in the theological academy and the church today. Some of his words and phrases have become part of our common Christian language, such as "cheap grace" to describe a confession of faith without corresponding biblical obedience and "costly grace" to explain a lifestyle of obedience that actively corresponds with a confession of faith. Bonhoeffer leaves behind a witness of opposition to Christianity regulated by an understanding of the Bible as unattainable high ideals. That Christianity was central to the problem of Christian apathy to Nazi racism. Instead, Bonhoeffer insisted that Christianity take seriously the life of Jesus, seeing discipleship as concrete historical action in obedience to the way of Jesus in Scripture and Christ's commandments as guidance for daily life—the difference for Bonhoeffer between cheap grace and costly grace. Bonhoeffer's radical Christian obedience to the point of death shows an inspirational witness of a life committed to costly grace.

BONHOEFFER AND THE PROBLEM OF RACE

Bonhoeffer remains the only prominent white theologian of the twentieth century to speak about racism as a Christian problem. As a white man, Bonhoeffer had access to multiple audiences in opposition to racial discrimination that were not available to people of color, and he appropriated what he learned in Harlem for that purpose. The black Jesus became a discursive figure representing God with and for the despised and rejected of all humanity. In America, Bonhoeffer found that the despised and rejected were black people. The demand for recognition by African Americans in the Harlem Renaissance was a demand for justice that can only come with the acknowledgment of their cohumanity, and Bonhoeffer's emphasis on being with and for others as a theological concept included a social and psychological dynamic of humanizing others and interrupting their abuse. His final imprisonment and death was a direct result of his empathic insistence that the church come to the aid of social victims. In Harlem Bonhoeffer saw black Christians connecting with Christ as an unconditional obligation not in power and privilege but in suffering humanity. In Harlem, Bonhoeffer began learning to embrace Christ hidden in suffering as resistance to oppression. His new awareness of racism gave him unique insight into nationalism as the racialized mixture of God and country embodied in idealized Aryan humanity. That reality included Christian identity synthesized into an untenable way of being in the world and of viewing self and others in it. Harlem provided what he needed to see the world differently and to imagine a different way of being a Christian within it.

The emphasis on incarnation and empathy in Bonhoeffer's prosocial theology was the key to his time in Harlem that opened him to new developments in his understanding of himself as a Christian German. His experience had an unforeseen effect of healthy self-evaluation and revision in his Christian identity in New York; he no longer blended Christianity and nation but seeing Christianity as an identity that transcends nation, in being with and for others, as blacks in Harlem transcended nation, being with and for others who were subject to white supremacy on the underside of the global color line.

Bonhoeffer remains relevant today, decades after his death, as a prophetic voice passionately calling Christians to live faithful lives in obedience to Christ. Retrieving Bonhoeffer's witness for guidance today may not lead to martyrdom, but it should lead to inspiration and some important correctives for contemporary Christians. As a prophetic figure, he demonstrates hope that the gospel does not remain forever captive to the diseased synthesis of nation and religion; he saw the problem and spent the rest of his life wrestling to uncouple nation and Christianity in his own identity as a white, Western, privileged Christian and in the understanding of Christianity in Germany during the Nazi era. He describes the cure to the problem of a diseased Christian imagination and the key to Christian discipleship as empathic, incarnational action on behalf of others. For Bonhoeffer, Christians must see society from the perspective of marginalized people since faithful Christianity is calibrated from the perspective of suffering rather than from dominance. This is costly yet crucial to true Christian discipleship. Bonhoeffer's legacy leaves an example of true discipleship. It led to his twentieth-century martyrdom, but it serves as inspiration for all who desire to unite with Christ in a world where justice rolls down like the waters. And he learned it from the black Christ in Harlem.

NOTES

INTRODUCTION

1   Victoria Barnett, *For the Soul of the People: Prostestant Protest against Hitler* (New York: Oxford University Press, 1992), 198–200.

2   Willie James Jennings, *The Christian Imagination: Theology and the Origins of Race* (New Haven, Conn.: Yale University Press, 2010), 8.

3   Psychologist Martin L. Hoffman describes empathy as "the vicarious affective response to another person." Hoffman's definition clarifies that empathy gets us into another person's context by including the following: "[it] is the involvement of psychological processes that make a person have feelings that are more congruent with another's situation than with his [or her] own situation." The awareness of an other's feelings is the entryway into an other's social context, and perhaps even that other's worldview, but an appropriate use of empathy is not imbalanced; it should not cause us to lose sight of our self as distinct from the other; it should allow us insight into the other's experience. The notion of empathy has implications for psychotherapy as well as psychological inquiry into the development of prosocial behavior. What I am interested in here is a link between moral psychologies and Christian ethics. Martin L. Hoffman, *Empathy and Moral Development: Implications for Caring and Justice* (Cambridge: Cambridge University Press, 2000), 29.

4   Saidiya V. Hartman, *Scenes of Subjection: Terror, Slavery, and Self-Making in Nineteenth-Century America*, Oxford University Press online (New York: Oxford University Press, 1999), 4.

5   I am not arguing that Bonhoeffer abandoned his loyalty to Germany or the German people. By paying attention to his loyalties, he corrected

141

the order of his allegiances and allowed his primary allegiance to Christ to speak into all other loyalties and passions with authority, so that his understanding of Christ did not remain co-opted by hidden, deviant, and deforming loyalties.

6   Lisa Cahill and Michael Walzer are scholars whose work connects with the language of empathy within their respective disciplines. Cahill, a Christian ethicist, advocates an inductive method of analysis. She describes a "practice-based approach to moral discernment" in the place of abstract, impartial reasoning. She advocates that we do our reasoning from concrete, practical experiences of injustice and well-being to make "revisable evaluative judgments" about human flourishing. According to Cahill, we recognize injustices in an other's context because of experiences of injustice in our own, as a tacit universalism. Michael Walzer is a political philosopher who also advocates an inductive analysis. Walzer describes what he calls a *moral minimalism*, the "reiterated features of our thick maximal moralities." A thick maximal morality is what we learn in our formative community, where we know the language of injustice and well-being in a particular way. Moral minimalism is the thin language of our public discourse that provides a minimal account of our particular, complex, fully developed maximal morality. Minimalism, unlike impartial reason, is not a claim to abstract or absolute universals; it is a cross-cultural language that remains intimately bound to the history and formation of its particular community. Cahill's and Walzer's more realistic ethical discourse about universals provides us with the means of reflecting on empathic experiences, moves from the particular to the universal, and corrects the misleading—universal to particular—approach of impartial reasoning. Cahill's notion of a practice-based approach to justice and peacemaking and Walzer's moral minimalism, taken together, delineate an inductive process that reiterates features of morality formed within the shared life of a community in a way that other communities can understand. It is also open to revisable evaluative judgments in the practice of pursuing the justice we are familiar with, in fresh awareness of a justice we are introduced to and against the injustice we know and meet in another context.

7   In a thus far unpublished translation, David Carl Stassen and Glen Harold Stassen argue that Bonhoeffer's famous term *Stellvertretung* may be translated as "representation," "action on behalf of," "deputyship," or "vicarious representative action." But in Bonhoeffer's writings it has a deeper theological connotation—not only of representing someone in a distant place where that person is not present, as a congressional representative does in the Capitol, but also of stepping into others' shoes, entering empathically into their place, and acting on their behalf with love. It contains the word *Stelle*, "place," and the word *treten*, "to step," like *eintreten*, "to enter into another's place" (a word Bonhoeffer often uses of Christ's *entering into* the center of our lives). So Bonhoeffer writes: "Christus . . . steht an ihrer Stelle [Christ stands in their place], stellvertretend für sie vor Gott [stepping into their place before God, or representing them before God]." It connotes being-with-each-other and being-for-each-other, entering into the other's reality and even the other's guilt. It is grounded in Bonhoeffer's christological emphasis

on the incarnation as God's *empathically entering into human life* in Jesus Christ, standing in the place of all humanity, and on the crucifixion as Christ's *bearing guilt on our behalf.* Christ's entering into our life incarnationally changes our reality. So Glen Stassen proposes that we translate *Stellvertretung* as "empathic representative action" or "incarnational representation." Bonhoeffer acted with empathic representation on behalf of Jews and other victims of Hitler's wars and Hitler's violence against the right to bodily life.

8   The emphasis that Bonhoeffer places on the incarnational and the empathic helps avoid the pitfalls of harmful universals and the tribalism of radical relativism. Yet there remains a need for a universal language. A healthy universal language involves attention to the ways different people experience life and acquire theological knowledge within their social location and context. Hoffman's work with empathy describes what he calls *empathic distress,* which is a sense of dis-ease caused by empathizing with someone in discomfort, pain, danger, or experiencing injustice, and his work can help in our effort to communicate across cultures in a healthy universal language. The attention brought to the civil rights movement in 1963 by the police brutality inflicted with fire hoses, night sticks, and attack dogs on nonviolent protesters in Birmingham, Alabama, is a historical example of the media aiding the movement to instigate empathic distress on a wider population.

CHAPTER ONE

1   Dietrich Bonhoeffer, *Barcelona, Berlin, New York: 1928–1931,* English ed., Dietrich Bonhoeffer Works (Minneapolis: Fortress, 2008), 10:412ff. Hereafter cited as DBWE.

2   DBWE 10:412ff.

3   In June 1919, the Allied countries that defeated Germany met with Germany in Versailles, France, where they forced Germany to sign a peace agreement. The Versailles peace agreement stipulated that Germany accept "sole guilt" for the war. See Eric Ames, Marcia Klotz, and Lora Wildenthal, *Germany's Colonial Pasts, Texts and Contexts* (Lincoln: University of Nebraska Press, 2005), 140–41.

4   Wolf-Dieter Zimmermann and Ronald Gregor Smith, *I Knew Dietrich Bonhoeffer,* 1st ed. (New York: Harper & Row, 1966), 42.

5   The Moravian Church in Herrnhut, Germany, was also influential for Bonhoeffer's mother's Christianity, and she was sure to pass it along to her children. See John W. de Gruchy, *The Cambridge Companion to Dietrich Bonhoeffer,* Cambridge Companions to Religion (Cambridge: Cambridge University Press, 1999), 24.

6   Bonhoeffer's cousin Christophe von Hase makes a connection between Walter's death, his parent's grief, and Bonhoeffer's very early decision to study theology. See DBWE 10:590, 591, 592.

7   Christophe von Hase followed Dietrich as a Sloane Fellow at Union in 1933. He remembered as a child being surprised at how his cousin was able to decide so early to study theology "and remain so unswervingly true to that decision." Dietrich's brothers tried to persuade him that the church was an incorrigibly feeble institution and that he was "taking the

path of least resistance," to which Dietrich replied, "In that case I shall reform it!" See DBWE 10:588.

8   Dietrich Bonhoeffer, *The Young Bonhoeffer*, DBWE (Minneapolis: Fortress, 2002), 9:60.

9   Ferdinand Schlingensiepen, *Dietrich Bonhoeffer, 1906–1945: Martyr, Thinker, Man of Resistance* (London: T&T Clark, 2010), 27.

10 Michael P. Dejonge, *Bonhoeffer's Theological Formation: Berlin, Barth, and Protestant Theology* (Oxford: Oxford University Press, 2012), 4.

11 Holl made a name for himself as the foremost Lutheran scholar of his era with his commemorative lecture, "What did Luther Understand by Religion?," and his subsequent publication of a number of essays on Luther. De Gruchy, *Cambridge Companion*, 56–57.

12 Eberhard Bethge, *Dietrich Bonhoeffer: A Biography*, rev. ed. (Minneapolis: Fortress, 2000), 70.

13 See M. Rumscheidt, ed., *Adolf von Harnack: Liberal Theology at Its Height* (London: Collins, 1989).

14 Of the three old-guard Berlin theologians, Professor Adolph Von Harnack (1851–1930) helped to forge a theological connection between religion and culture by seeking to grasp the essence of faith, free from its historical particularity, for historical engagement and to endorse a cultured "person of reason and faith." Bonhoeffer was also greatly influenced early by Karl Holl's (1866–1926) "Luther Renaissance." Holl interpreted Luther's doctrine of justification, *simul justus et peccator* (humans are simultaneously sinners and justified) to describe a paradoxical integration of the justice and love of God. This was an interpretation that described Lutheranism as a "religion of conscience." But the influence of Karl Barth was already strong in Bonhoeffer's theology by the time he sat as a Ph.D. student in class with Karl Holl, and Bonhoeffer could not accept Holl's "religion of conscience" assessment of Lutheranism, seeing in it a human claim upon God's revelation, rather than knowledge of God as an act of God's self-revelation alone. But Holl's reference to justification encountered by grace as a gift from God through the church left its mark on Bonhoeffer. The third member of the old guard was Bonhoeffer's dissertation advisor, professor Reinhold Seeberg (1859–1935). Seeberg was also a historical theologian whose five-volume *Textbook of the History of Doctrines* contained some of the theological works that Bonhoeffer most relied upon very early in his theological studies. Seeberg contributed not only to Bonhoeffer's theological language of sociality but also to the way in which Bonhoeffer came to see theology as a function of the church, as a concrete revelation of Christ in the world. Together, Harnack, Holl, and Seeberg gave to Bonhoeffer a theology that was social, historically concrete, Lutheran, and Christ centered. See Bethge, *Dietrich Bonhoeffer*; de Gruchy, *Cambridge Companion*; Dejonge, *Bonhoeffer's Theological Formation*; Rumscheidt, *Adolf von Harnack*.

15 Keith Clements explains orders of creation as "the doctrine that certain structures of human life are not just incidental biological or historical phenomena but are deliberately ordained of God as essential and immutable conditions of human existence, without which humanity is not humanity as created by God." Clements claims that the term was in

broad usage but it took a definitively pernicious turn in its use by emerging German National Socialists, who claimed, "Above all *the* supreme order of creation is the people, race, or nation to which one belongs and owes loyalty." The use of "orders" language here is protonationalist, speaking of loyalty to *Volk* in a way that presaged the National Socialist usage that was on the horizon. See de Gruchy, *Cambridge Companion*, 163. A similar usage of orders of creation language was appropriated in the slave-owning south to argue for the innate superiority of men over women and of white people in general over other "inferior" races, in accordance with God's divine created order. See Beth Barton Schweiger, *Religion in the American South: Protestants and Others in History and Culture* (Chapel Hill: University of North Carolina Press, 2003) 285–91; and Richard Furman's "Defense of Slavery," in *Exploring the Christian Heritage: A Reader in History and Theology*, ed. C. Douglas Weaver, Rady Roldán-Figueroa, Brandon Frick (Waco, Tex.: Baylor University Press, 2012), 154–57.

16   The language of blood and soil was a German emphasis on pure ethnicity, tied to geography and *Volk* heritage. Bonhoeffer made use of themes introduced in *Sanctorum Communio*, including Christ the *Stellvertretung*. As "the one for others," Christ is free *for* humankind, not free *from* humankind, as the early Karl Barth had indicated. In Christ, God's transcendence comes to us as a person and makes ethical claims on humanity in social interaction with one another. Christ the *Stellvertretung* stands in for us, freeing us from bondage to self that would otherwise prohibit us from relationship with God, and enabling us to be free for others. But at this early developmental stage, he is struggling with popular ideology within his theology.

17   DBWE 10:343.

18   The language of *Völker* is translated as folk, peoples, or nation, but its meaning is more complex in the German, as the excerpt from "Basic Questions of a Christian Ethic" illustrates. It has connotations of a national essence, or people's spirit. In the eighteenth century, Johann Gottfried Herder developed the concept of a German *Volksgeist* (national spirit) to describe the natural, hereditary, or ethnic grouping to which every people belongs as a reason for political distinctiveness. His argument also spoke of the pride of the distinctive German *Volksgeist* within the German *Völker*. Bonhoeffer's language in these two lectures espouses this language of loyalty to *Völker* as it is appropriated within popular nationalist theology. See note 32 in DBWE 10:337, 371–72.

19   This is a reference to *Lebensraum* (living space), which was a key National Socialist concept motivating the Nazi military advance across Europe.

20   The notion that God calls peoples, a notion that has biblical roots, was a means of countering the humiliation and distressing conditions in post–World War I Germany. The terms of peace agreed upon within the 1919 Treaty of Versailles were perceived with deep indignation as the "pushing aside" of the German people. The distress of one's own people became a recurring, common theme. See DBWE 10:373n34, 339–42.

21   The *theologia crucis* refers to the location of the revelation of Christ in history and the source from which theology is understood, thus

corresponding with Bonhoeffer's argument that God is revealed in Christ, as the communion of saints.

22   Later, in his prison letters, Bonhoeffer advocates a "religionless Christianity," indicating continuity in his perspective on religion. I am arguing as Bonhoeffer did, that at this early stage his argument about faithful Christianity did not include the Bible as a concrete guide for Christian living, which had a negative effect on his still-developing theological worldview. His advocacy for a religionless Christianity in prison had developed an insistence on biblical concreteness that was not present at this early developmental stage in Berlin. See DBWE 10:353.

23   DBWE 10:354.

24   DBWE 10:365.

25   The language of the *theologia crucis* speaks about the revelation of God in suffering. It is an irony that God should not reveal God's self in glory but in Christ, that God's self-revelation happened in suffering. Here in Barcelona, the language of God revealed in suffering has not caught Bonhoeffer's attention yet. That did not occur before he found a congregation that demonstrated his theological description of Christ existing as church-community at Abyssinian Baptist Church in Harlem.

26   Clifford J. Green, *Bonhoeffer: A Theology of Sociality*, rev. ed. (Grand Rapids: Eerdmans, 1999), 127.

27   DBWE 10:362.

28   Hienz Tödt claims that some of the themes within the Lutheran revival, what he describes as "neo-Lutheranism," espoused the nationalism that we see here, where love for one's people sanctifies killing. "Here [Bonhoeffer] argues indeed in line with neo-Lutheran tradition. . . . According to Bonhoeffer's judgment then, to interpret the command as pacifism on principle does not fit in with God's real will for this specific situation, since such an interpretation is not concrete . . . participation in the war of one's own Volk, even [when] it must [initiate] aggression for the sake of its historical growth, in the conviction that it thereby is following God's guidance of history." See Heinz Eduard Tödt, Ernst-Albert Scharffenorth, and Glen Harold Stassen, *Authentic Faith: Bonhoeffer's Theological Ethics in Context*, English ed. (Grand Rapids: Eerdmans, 2007), 80.

29   DBWE 10:371.

30   This is how Bonhoeffer ended his second lecture, "The Essence of Christianity." The ending calls to mind the Emperor Constantine commanding his troops to place the sign of the cross on their shields as they head into battle, when Bonhoeffer says, "German people, that is your God, the God who formed you and will abide with you. In your struggles with fate, keep your eyes on the cross, the most powerful wonderful emblem of your God, and be assured that only in this sign will you be victorious!" DBWE 10:322, 359.

31   Bethge, *Dietrich Bonhoeffer*, 120.

32   See DBWE 10:265, as quoted in Hans Pfeifer, "Learning Faith and Ethical Commitment in the Context of Spiritual Training Groups: Consequenses of Dietrich Bonhoeffer's Post Doctoral Year in New York City 1930/31," *Dietrich Bonhoeffer Jahrbuch 3 / Dietrich Bonhoeffer Yearbook 3* (2007/2008): 253.

33   Pfeifer, "Learning Faith and Ethical Commitment," 254.
34   I am appropriating this idea about the early stages of Bonhoeffer's theological career in the same manner that the late German Bonhoeffer scholar Hans Pfeifer has done in his masterful essay, "Learning Faith and Ethical Commitment," 257.
35   Pfeifer, "Learning Faith and Ethical Commitment," 257.
36   Bethge, *Dietrich Bonhoeffer*, 157.
37   See Clifford Green's introduction as editor, DBWE 10:19.
38   DBWE 10:22.
39   DBWE 10:309.
40   DBWE 10:310.
41   DBWE 10:265.
42   In his report about his Sloane Fellowship, Bonhoeffer made mention of the role of pragmatism for the modern American. The problem had to do, as Bonhoeffer described it, with a blend of religion and faith in progress that saw no value in theological language that deals with anything that is not instrumental, or does not "work." Validity is not the criterion for truth; truth becomes what works to advance life, culture, and civilization. With workability as the criteria, American pragmatists had no use for the dogmatics or Lutheranism that Bonhoeffer held so dear. Bonhoeffer described them as Pelagian (the heresy that holds that "human effort, in addition to God's grace, contributes essentially to human salvation") and adherents of Protagoras (the fifth-century-BCE Greek philosopher who said that the human being is the measure of all things). See DBWE 10:269–70.
43   Bonhoeffer's professors at Berlin, people like Adolf von Harnack, were among some of the founding members of theological liberalism. Gary Dorrien argues that the founders of American academic theological liberalism conceded that German universities and scholarship were superior and that some of the contributors to the American version of theological liberalism were directly schooled by German philosophy or biblical scholarship. Yet American theological liberalism was also indigenous to the environment, as Bonhoeffer discovered, and heavily influenced by pragmatism, Scottish Common Sense philosophy, and Unitarian thinkers. The content of the American and the German forms of liberal theology were vastly different. See Gary J. Dorrien, *The Making of American Liberal Theology: Imagining Progressive Religion, 1805–1900*, 1st ed. (Louisville, Ky.: Westminster John Knox, 2001), xvii. And see Bonhoeffer's *Report on His Year of Study Prepared for the Church Federation Office*, DBWE 10:305–19.
44   DBWE 10:313.
45   DBWE 10:313–14.
46   DBWE 10:313–14.
47   Dorrien, *Making of American Liberal Theology*, xix.
48   In his end-of-the-year report to the Church Federation Office, Bonhoeffer wrote about a visit to an Episcopal church in New York on Good Friday, 1931, to listen to a renowned preacher (probably William Norman Guthrie, who was the rector of the Manhattan Episcopal church St. Marks in-the-Bouwerie from 1911–1937). Bonhoeffer was shocked to hear the preacher proclaim, "I deny the reconciliation on the cross; I don't want that kind of Christ." See DBWE 10:276–77.

49 Dorrien, *Making of American Liberal Theology*, xiv.

50 See Dorrien, *Making of American Liberal Theology*, xiii.

51 Deitrich Bonhoeffer to Max Deistel, November 5, 1942, DBWE 16:367–68.

52 See Green's introduction, DBWE 10:25.

53 See DBWE 10:25ff.

54 Empathy, as I am using it, suggests the ability to share in the experience of another person, to enter their context with the ability to reflect on the concrete needs for justice there, without losing grasp on our own separate identities. I am describing empathy as a prosocial, inductive encounter with others, yet I am aware that the language of the empathic social encounter is not without significant problems. For our purposes here, psychologist Martin L. Hoffman describes empathy as "the vicarious affective response to another person." Hoffman, *Empathy and Moral Development*, 29.

55 I am tremendously thankful to the family of Albert Franklin Fisher for numerous phone conversations, during which they shared with me all the family history that I am discussing here, specifically, Albert Fisher's daughters, Valerie Fisher and Judy Arrington, who were children when their father passed away at age sixty-two, and his niece Minnie Rose Jay-Richardson, who was in her teen years when her uncle Al passed away. I have had the privilege of being welcomed by their wonderful family as if I were one of their relatives.

56 Anthony Richardson's great-granddaughter, Minnie Rose Richardson, graciously shared stories with me of her great-grandfather. Her stories correlate with the research done by Eric C. Lincoln about the role of the black church in the African American experience. See Edward Franklin Frazier and C. Eric Lincoln, *The Negro Church in America*, Sourcebooks in Negro History (New York: Schocken, 1974).

57 The Baptist Theological Union and Baptist Union Theological Seminary eventually became the Chicago Divinity School. See Wilson Fallin, *The African American Church in Birmingham, Alabama, 1815–1963: A Shelter in the Storm*, Studies in African American History and Culture (New York: Garland, 1997), 90.

58 One of Albert Fisher's nieces, Lisa Richardson, is a journalist and uncovered this history of Albert's father, Charles, as she was doing research on their family. See Richardson, "Going Back to Find Lavinia," *LA Times*, January 16, 2000, http://articles.latimes.com/2000/jan/16/news/mn-54631/7.

59 Larry O. Rivers, "Our God Is Marching On: James Hudson and the Theological Foundation of the Civil Rights Movement" (Ph.D. diss., Vanderbilt University, 2010).

60 Albert lived with his family in Hartford for six years of his childhood, from ages eight to fourteen, until he left home to attend the college preparatory high school connected to Morehouse College in Atlanta. After Morehouse prep, he attended Howard College in Washington, D.C., where he earned his B.A. in the summer of 1930.

61 Manfred Berg, *Popular Justice: A History of Lynching in America*, The American Ways Series (Chicago: Ivan R. Dee, 2011), 92.

62 On August 7, 1930, Shipp, eighteen, and Smith, nineteen, were arrested in Marion, Indiana, and charged with rape and murder. Shortly after their arrest, they were dragged from the sheriff's jail by a white mob, brutally tortured, and lynched. They became the last confirmed lynching in the northern United States. See James Cameron, *A Time of Terror* (Milwaukee, Wis.: TD Publications, 1982), 49–63.

63 James H. Madison, *A Lynching in the Heartland: Race and Memory in America*, 1st ed. (New York: Palgrave, 2001), 113.

64 DBWE 10:29.

65 On April 19, 2013, Alabama Governor Robert Bentley signed a bill posthumously pardoning all nine of the Scottsboro boys of any and all wrongdoing, eighty years after their racially motivated wrongful convictions.

66 See Dietrich Bonhoeffer, *Ethics*, DBWE (Minneapolis: Fortress, 2005), 6:295, as quoted by Clifford Green in *Bonhoeffer*, 29, 30.

67 Howard Thurman and Vincent Harding, *Jesus and the Disinherited* (Boston, Mass.: Beacon, 1996), 36–57.

68 Nathan Irvin Huggins, *Harlem Renaissance* (London: Oxford University Press, 1973), 15.

69 Alain LeRoy Locke, *The New Negro: An Interpretation* (New York: Johnson, 1968), 6. The term "New Negro" was in public use long before it appeared in Locke's collection. As early as 1900, Booker T. Washington appropriated the term for a collection of essays that he coedited. See Booker T. Washington, Fannie Barrier Williams, and Norman Barton Wood, *A New Negro for a New Century: An Accurate and Up-to-Date Record of the Upward Struggles of the Negro Race* (Chicago: American, 1900).

70 Huggins, *Harlem Renaissance*, 15.

71 James Weldon Johnson was the first African American executive secretary of the NAACP and another significant architect of the Harlem Renaissance movement. As executive secretary, Johnson was in charge of the NAACP. See Henry Louis Gates, Evelyn Brooks Higginbotham, and American Council of Learned Societies, *Harlem Renaissance Lives from the African American National Biography* (Oxford: Oxford University Press, 2009), 297–99.

72 See James Weldon Johnson, *Black Manhattan* (New York: A. A. Knopf, 1930), xiii.

73 Here again I want to emphasize that it is misleading to say that Bonhoeffer saw the world as if he were a black person. Empathy does not mean that we evacuate ourselves when we see from an other's perspective; empathy makes us have feelings that are more congruent with an other's situation than with our own. It allows us insight to an other's experience while we remain ourselves with our accumulated history. A healthy practice of empathy reveals something from the other's perspective that comes to the empathic person as new content. See Hoffman, *Empathy and Moral Development*, 29–30; and DBWE 10:314.

74 DBWE 10:315.

75 DBWE 10:313.

76 DBWE 10:313.

77 DBWE 10:315.

78   Ruth Zerner, "Dietrich Bonhoeffer's American Experiences: People, Letters, and Papers from Union Seminary," *Union Seminary Quarterly Review* 31, no. 4 (1976): 268.

79   This is a theme that runs throughout the argument in James H. Cone's masterful work, *The Cross and the Lynching Tree* (Maryknoll, N.Y.: Orbis Books, 2011), 18, 88.

80   Dorothee Sölle, *Suffering* (Philadelphia: Fortress, 1975), 22–32.

81   Cone, *Cross and the Lynching Tree*, 21.

82   James Weldon Johnson, J. Rosamond Johnson, and Lawrence Brown, *The Books of American Negro Spirituals: Including the Book of American Negro Spirituals and the Second Book of Negro Spirituals* (New York: Da Capo, 1977), ii, 136.

83   Cone, *Cross and the Lynching Tree*, 18.

84   DBWE 10:314–15.

85   Myles Horton was a staunch advocate of the civil rights movement and cofounder of the Highlander Folk School, which specializes in social justice leadership. Notable leaders of the civil rights movement like Rosa Parks, Martin Luther King Jr., Ralph Abernathy, and James Lewis received training at Horton's school. But prior to his work in the civil rights movement, Horton was a student with Bonhoeffer at Union. Frank Adams and Myles Horton, *Unearthing Seeds of Fire: The Idea of Highlander* (Winston-Salem, N.C.: J. F. Blair, 1975), 148.

86   DBWE 10:31.

87   DBWE 10:31.

88   DBWE 10:199.

89   Zimmermann and Smith, *I Knew Dietrich Bonhoeffer*, 47.

90   Bethge, *Dietrich Bonhoeffer*, 152ff.

91   Bethge, *Dietrich Bonhoeffer*, 154.

92   Dietrich Bonhoeffer, *Letters and Papers from Prison*, DBWE 8:486. Schlingensiepen explains that a post–World War II conversation with Lasserre revealed that the conversation in which Bonhoeffer understood him to say that he hoped to be a saint was in fact a problem of translation. For both men, English was a second language and Lasserre's real intent to say that he hoped to live a life "sanctified by consistently following God's commandments" was lost in translation. See Schlingensiepen, *Dietrich Bonhoeffer, 1906–1945*, 73.

93   Pfeifer, "Learning Faith and Ethical Commitment," 263.

94   Zimmermann and Smith, *I Knew Dietrich Bonhoeffer*, 47.

95   See the editor's introduction to DBWE 10:26.

96   Pfeifer, "Learning Faith and Ethical Commitment," 263.

97   See Green's introduction to DBWE 10:26–27.

98   See Green's introduction to DBWE 10:27.

99   Jean Lasserre, *War and the Gospel* (Scottdale, Pa.,: Herald, 1962), 71.

100   DBWE 10:368.

101   Lasserre, *War and the Gospel*, 14. In an interview featured in Martin Doblmeier's documentary on Bonhoeffer, Lasserre verified that this was indeed the content of conversations that he had with Bonhoeffer. See Martin Doblmeier's documentary "Bonhoeffer: Pastor, Pacifist, Nazi Resister."

102   DBWE 10:363.

103 DBWE 10:363.
104 Lasserre, *War and the Gospel*, 71, emphasis added.
105 Lasserre, *War and the Gospel*, 71–72.
106 Dietrich Bonhoeffer, *Discipleship*, DBWE (Minneapolis: Fortress, 2003), 4:39.
107 Dietrich Bonhoeffer, *Berlin: 1932–1933*, DBWE (Minneapolis: Fortress, 2009), 12:258–62.
108 DBWE 4:51.
109 DBWE 4:44.
110 Matt 5:15.
111 DBWE 4:113.

CHAPTER TWO

1   Bonhoeffer completed his second dissertation and was also candidate for ordination in the German Lutheran Church. But regardless of his academic accomplishments, he was one year shy of the required age of twenty-five for ordination. Bonhoeffer's church superintendent, Max Diestel, recommended that the young scholar "look around the world a bit first" before being ordained and assuming his post at the University of Berlin. Diestel recommended that Bonhoeffer travel to America for his studies. See DBWE 10:200.
2   See Bethge, *Dietrich Bonhoeffer*, 143.
3   Bethge, *Dietrich Bonhoeffer*, 143.
4   DBWE 10:199.
5   DBWE 10:199.
6   Shamoon Zamir, *The Cambridge Companion to W.E.B. Du Bois*, Cambridge Companions to American Studies (Cambridge: Cambridge University Press, 2008), 265.
7   Locke, *New Negro*, 6.
8   The term "lynch law" was a colloquialism that historians recognize as referring to the very real Colonel Charles Lynch (1736–1796) of Bedford County, Virginia, for his socially accepted practice of punishment outside of the law. During the American Revolution, Colonel Lynch presided over extralegal courts that claimed to fight lawlessness in general and the activities of British Loyalists in particular. Colonel Lynch himself used the term "Lynchs [*sic*] law" in reference to irregular punishment. The lynch law was popular justice, used to terrorize African Americans, and was generally accepted extralegal capital punishment. See Berg, *Popular Justice*, 3.
9   Locke, *New Negro*, 6. Also see Isabel Wilkerson's fantastic work on the Great Migration, *The Warmth of Other Suns: The Epic Story of America's Great Migration*, 1st ed. (New York: Random House, 2010).
10 Michelle Ann Stephens, *Black Empire: The Masculine Global Imaginary of Caribbean Intellectuals in the United States, 1914–1962*, New Americanists (Durham, N.C.: Duke University Press, 2005), 40.
11 Locke, *New Negro*.
12 Du Bois begins his groundbreaking book *The Souls of Black Folk* by describing the problem of the color line, a power structure that belts the

planet, subjugating people of color to whites-only power structures. It is also reinforced by an abstract theology that gives theological support to an ideal humanity, providing theological justification for social evil in daily interaction. See W.E.B. Du Bois, *The Souls of Black Folk*, Bantam classic ed. (New York: Bantam, 1989), 1.

13 DBWE 10:321.

14 Adam Clayton Powell Sr. was senior pastor of Abyssinian Baptist Church during Bonhoeffer's time in attendance there. Powell often referred to faithful Christianity as applied Christianity, betraying the influence of the social gospel movement on his interpretation of Christian faithfulness. It's most likely that Powell was referencing the popular book by the prominent social gospel architect Washington Gladden. See Washington Gladden, *Applied Christianity: Moral Aspects of Social Questions* (Boston: Houghton Riverside Press, 1899).

15 DBWE 10:318, 420.

16 DBWE 10:318.

17 Bethge, *Dietrich Bonhoeffer*, 162.

18 DBWE 10:320.

19 This may be a reference to the YMCA that was located on W. 135th Street in Harlem. It was around the block from Abyssinian Baptist Church, which is located on W. 136th. In addition to his role in the community at Abyssinian, Bonhoeffer was making weekly visits to the YMCA in Harlem, which exposed him to the broader community of youth there. See DBWE 10:318, 320.

20 The Association for the Advancement of Colored People is a reference to the NAACP. See DBWE 10:318.

21 DBWE 10:428.

22 Bethge, *Dietrich Bonhoeffer*, 163.

23 Bethge, *Dietrich Bonhoeffer*, 229.

24 Bethge, *Dietrich Bonhoeffer*.

25 DBWE 10:265.

26 DBWE 10:265.

27 DBWE 10:266.

28 Walter Mignolo, *The Idea of Latin America*, Blackwell Manifestos (Malden, Mass.; Oxford: Blackwell, 2005), 8.

29 DBWE 10:315.

30 I am drawing on an argument from Marcia Klotz's fantastic essay "The Weimar Republic: A Postcolonial State in a Still Colonial World." Klotz argues that after World War I, Germany feared being colonized by the community of empires in which it was situated. As a postcolonial state in a still-colonial world, Germany was forced to negotiate its identity in opposition to its neighbors. See Ames, Klotz, and Wildenthal, *Germany's Colonial Pasts*, 135.

31 In compliance with the stipulations of the Versailles Peace Treaty of 1919, Germany was stripped of all of its colonial possessions and lost its status as a fellow imperial power in a European community of states that retained colonial possessions. See Ames, Klotz, and Wildenthal, *Germany's Colonial Pasts*.

32 DBWE 12:95.

33 See Jennings, *Christian Imagination*.

34 Jennings, *Christian Imagination*, 114.
35 See Zerner, "Bonhoeffer's American Experiences," 262.
36 Mignolo, *Idea of Latin America*, 35.
37 See Sara Friedrichsmeyer, Sara Lennox, and Susanne Zantop, *The Imperialist Imagination: German Colonialism and Its Legacy*, Social History, Popular Culture, and Politics in Germany (Ann Arbor: University of Michigan Press, 1998), 23–24.
38 See Edward W. Said, *Orientalism*, 25th anniversary ed. (New York: Vintage Books, 2003), 3, 8.
39 This is a description of social imagination coined by Edward Said. Said's description of Orientalism sounds similar to Jennings' account of a social imagination and the structures responsible for the assembly of a diseased one in the West: "Orientalism can be discussed and analyzed as the corporate institution for dealing with the Orient—dealing with it by making statements about it, authorizing views of it, describing it, teaching it, settling it, ruling over it. [It is] a detailed logic governed . . . by a battery of desires, repressions, investments, and projections. . . . The Orient is the construct of a European ideal; an abstract social imagination assembled in the imperial West as they made contact with eastern foreigners, through discourse about self in contradistinction to those foreign 'oriental' others." Said, *Orientalism*, 3.
40 I am not suggesting that Germany had colonial possessions in Asia, the Middle East, or North Africa or that they were participants in the late eighteenth-century Orientalizing efforts of the British and the French. Indeed, Germany as a nation-state did not exist until 1871 (see Nina Berman, "Orientalism, Imperialism, and Nationalism: Karl May's *Orientzyklus*," in Friedrichsmeyer, Lennox, and Zantop, *Imperialist Imagination*, 52). I am referring to the Oriental/Occidental process of European identity formation based on "othering." Yet, Nina Berman argues that Germany did practice Orientalism as an intellectual endeavor, but not one that occurred from colonial possessions in those places labeled "the Orient." In 1884 Germany claimed as their territories German Southwest Africa, German East Africa, Cameroon, and Togo. They remained German possessions until the end of World War I.
41 Ames, Klotz, and Wildenthal, *Germany's Colonial Pasts*, 124.
42 For pre– and post–World War I Germany, efforts toward an ideal race were derived from Nationalist Socialist notions of purity, defined as undiluted German blood. And in perfect alignment with the racializing practices of modern European imperialism, physical features, like skin color, were at times visible signs of the purity they sought. See Ames, Klotz, and Wildenthal, *Germany's Colonial Pasts*, 121.
43 Mignolo, *Idea of Latin America*, 35.
44 DBWE 10:39.
45 German colonialism had valued race and space, eugenicist ideas of racial selection, racial reproduction, and territorial expansion to develop the ideal racial order. See Ames, Klotz, and Wildenthal, *Germany's Colonial Pasts*, 118. It was based on what Karl Deutsch describes as "national consciousness," which is nurtured in the kind of forced isolation that results in the solidarity of a people. That same national consciousness,

especially the experience of isolation and solidarity, or separation and cohesion, was particularly acute in the post–World War I German experience of isolation and suffering. See Karl Wolfgang Deutsch, *Nationalism and Social Communication: An Inquiry into the Foundations of Nationality*, 2nd ed. (Cambridge, Mass.: MIT Press, 1966), 173.

46　The curse of Ham myth is a misrepresentation of Genesis 9:20-27, where Noah pronounces a curse on his grandson, Canaan, the son of Ham. The distortion came to be understood as a biblical curse on black people, since Ham was mythologically understood as the father of the darker races where the climate is hotter. If the curse was upon Canaan, as the passage is written, it could not be read as a patriarch's curse on African people and thus could not have become the biblical endorsement of perpetual race-based slavery. See George M. Fredrickson, *Racism: A Short History* (Princeton, N.J.: Princeton University Press, 2002), 42–45.

47　Mignolo illustrates the famous "T-in-O" map that was published in the ninth-century edition of Isiadore of Seville's *Etymologies*. The map demonstrates an obvious tripartite division, with Asia occupying the top part of the circle (in an emerging interpretation of the shape of the Earth), and Europe and Africa dividing among themselves the bottom half. This early division of the world, prior to the discovery of a fourth continent, provides the rationale for the later interpretation that the world is naturally divided into four continents—Asia, Africa, Europe, and America. Mignolo, *Idea of Latin America*, 23.

48　This European Christian geopolitical construct provided a connection among the continents where there was no natural connection. It was a pseudo-Christian connection that was based on a theological understanding of continents and their inhabitants—an order of creation—primarily paying attention to the roles of Ham and Japheth. According to Augustine, Shem was important as the ancestor of Semitic peoples, through whom Christ was born, while the destiny of Ham was marked by a curse, and Japheth was destined to expand.

49　Mignolo explains that there was no such natural connection among land masses and the sons of Noah in China, or within Islam, for example. The division of the world into land masses that corresponded with a son of Noah became the understanding of how the world was actually organized, and the T-in-O map was integrated into more sophisticated renderings of the world map, like the "Orbis Universalis Terrarum," the "Universal World" (c. 1575). See Mignolo, *Idea of Latin America*, 24, 25.

50　Jennings, *Christian Imagination*, 113. Non-European people were brought into a new worldview by force, grafted into the European body of Christ in a violent denial of the practice of incarnation and a reinterpretation of humanity as racialized flesh.

51　By "commodified bodies" I am referring to the use of people of color as forced labor within European colonial possessions, as well as the transatlantic slave trade. Bodies were subject to use by imperialists within the colonies as properties. But the transatlantic slave trade was the most obvious example of commodified bodies. Jennings, *Christian Imagination*, 58.

52　By "the practice of incarnation" Jennings is referring to the historically fluid, adaptable, even protean character of Christianity that could incarnationally enter cultures and lands and become a part of what was already there. It is a healthier intimacy that joins other non-Jewish cultures and people as gentiles in Israel's house, as participants in a relational understanding of Christian discipleship as Jennings describes.

> Incarnational logic here is not analogical but participatory; it is the logic of discipleship and mission, the going forth in the triune name. The denial of incarnational practice is precisely the failure to go forward as the Son came forward and wishes to go forward in intimate joining. . . . The destruction of the connections between native spatial logics and identities, the possibilities of cultural intimacy configured around landscape were never to be realized. Christian intellectual tradition in the New World denies its most fundamental starting point, that of the divine Word entering flesh in time and space to become Jewish flesh. The domination and authoritarianism that described a colonial order inverted the historical Christian worldview, and the natural sense of hospitality was inverted; wherever it went, the Christian/colonialist construct claimed to be the host and owner of the spaces it entered and demanded that the native peoples enter its worldview.

Jennings, *Christian Imagination*, 8, 113.

53 Jennings, *Christian Imagination*, 9.

54 Ames, Klotz, and Wildenthal, *Germany's Colonial Pasts*, 140.

55 The League of Nations was a governing body of nation-states assembled to help sort through the post–World War I disorder and keep the world safe from another global conflict. Klotz describes the League of Nations as "an international body to which grievances could be addressed if not necessarily acted upon." The mandate for its existence was written into the Treaty of Versailles, at the Versailles Peace Conference of 1919. See Ames, Klotz, and Wildenthal, *Germany's Colonial Pasts*, 141.

56 In particular, article 231 of that treaty made exacting claims of German responsibility for the war, stipulating that Germany admit sole guilt for starting the global conflict and destabilizing the world. Not only was the outcome devastating for their nation but Germans viewed the sole-guilt thesis in article 231 of the Versailles treaty as unjust. Bonhoeffer spoke about the treaty in 1930: "It can be proved historically, that the art. 231 of the treaty of Versailles is an injustice against our country and we have a right to protest. That fact is recognized by the largest parts of educated people in Europe and in America." Article 231 also stated that consequently they should pay a tremendous war debt every year for the next forty-seven years to the allies who defeated them. See DBWE 10:413n7 and DBWE 10:416n16.

57 Bonhoeffer implied that Germany was not the perpetrator of injustice but its victim. Indeed, the Treaty of Versailles was creating generations of victims: "It is impossible for us to provide social and economic conditions for our children in the future, in which we can trust for security. I must know that my grandchildren still will have to pay reparations and war debts." Bonhoeffer was not merely complaining about the Versailles treaty; by describing the situation in Germany and the German attitude toward the Treaty of Versailles, he was expressing his own empathic awareness of the post–World War I nationalistic reaction in Germany,

even pleading for Americans to be aware of the danger of the punitive attitude within the League of Nations toward Germany that was feeding the problematic German attitude toward other nations and asking for it to be changed. See DBWE 10:415.

58 Ames, Klotz, and Wildenthal, *Germany's Colonial Pasts*, 136.
59 See Benedict Anderson, *Imagined Communities*, as quoted by Stephens, *Black Empire*, 27.
60 People of the African diaspora, spread throughout the world as a result of the transatlantic slave trade, were most important to Bonhoeffer's experience of Harlem. The Great Migration and the global awareness of white supremacy were elements of a black consciousness that was emerging in Harlem during Bonhoeffer's visit there. Paul Gilroy, *The Black Atlantic: Modernity and Double Consciousness* (Cambridge, Mass.: Harvard University Press, 1993), 2.
61 Stephens, *Black Empire*, 36.
62 Coincidentally, the Bolshevik Revolution came to resolution in 1917, near the time that World War I was ending, and the Bolshevik leader, Vladimir Lenin, offered a proposal that included as a constituent of peace in Russia the liberation of all of Russia's colonies and the liberation of all dependent, oppressed, and nonsovereign peoples under Russian occupation. Lenin's Bolshevik plans for peace, rather than the Versailles plan, proved more attractive to the underside of the color line. See Vladimir Lenin, "Fourth Letter: How to Achieve Peace," as quoted in Ames, Klotz, and Wildenthal, *Germany's Colonial Pasts*, 140. Lenin's plan for peace occurred near the time of the Versailles Peace Conference, and it did not go unnoticed by leadership in the League. In particular, U.S. president Woodrow Wilson responded to Lenin's proposal by reiterating many of Lenin's proposals for peace in his famous "Fourteen Points," with an important caveat: Lenin's call to free colonized people was summarily ignored. A Japanese delegation made the same request for the freedom of colonized people at the 1919 meeting of the League of Nations in Versailles, only to receive the same denial. But these requests occurring within the discourse on world leadership by world leaders in the context of a global reorganization indicate that, despite continued loyalty to the white imperialist worldview, the ideological underpinnings of colonialism had been shaken by the war. See Ames, Klotz, and Wildenthal, *Germany's Colonial Pasts*, 141.
63 Stephens, *Black Empire*, 3.
64 I am including in this notion of the African diaspora all people caught on the unfavorable side of the color line. That is faithful to early twentieth-century use of the term "colored." It was not uncommon for dark-skinned people of non-African decent to be called by dysphemisms that were typically leveled at people of African descent.

CHAPTER THREE

1 Du Bois, *Souls of Black Folk*, 114.
2 Harlem Renaissance writer Arna Bontemps tells us that the black literary movement in Harlem consisted of two phases. Bontemps referred to

phase 1 as the period of black propaganda, which consisted of political themes and artwork intended to reframe the public image of African Americans. The propaganda stage (1921–1924) was a period that attracted talent to Harlem, and when they arrived the literary movement resulted in a second stage (1924–1931), that of a proliferation of black literature. The NAACP and the National Urban League were the essential supporters of the second stage literary movement with widely read magazines that published the works of talented black writers. See National Urban League, *The Opportunity Reader: Stories, Poetry, and Essays from the Urban League's "Opportunity" Magazine*, Modern Library Harlem Renaissance (New York: Modern Library, 1999), xvi.

3   Mignolo, *Idea of Latin America*, 9.

4   Du Bois graduated cum laude, with a B.A. on June 25, 1890, from Harvard University and completed a year of study toward his Ph.D. at the University of Berlin in 1892–1893. Du Bois celebrated his twenty-fifth birthday in February of that school year, before his funding source dried up, causing him to return to America, where in 1895 he became the first African American to receive a Ph.D. from Harvard. Bonhoeffer would celebrate his twenty-fifth birthday in America on February 4 as an exchange student thirty-eight years later. The University of Berlin was where Bonhoeffer received his Ph.D. in theology, and, upon his return from New York in 1931, he joined the faculty there.

5   David L. Lewis, *W.E.B. Du Bois: Biography of a Race, 1868–1919*, 1st ed. (New York: H. Holt, 1993), 561.

6   W.E.B. Du Bois, *Darkwater: Voices from within the Veil*, Dover Thrift Editions (Mineola, N.Y.: Dover, 1999), ix.

7   Edward J. Blum, *W.E.B. Du Bois: American Prophet*, Politics and Culture in Modern America (Philadelphia: University of Pennsylvania Press, 2007), 27.

8   Du Bois, *Darkwater*, ix.

9   DBWE 10:314.

10   Du Bois, *Souls of Black Folk*, 1ff.

11   See Jonathon Samuel Kahn, *Divine Discontent: The Religious Imagination of W.E.B. Du Bois* (Oxford: Oxford University Press, 2009), 25, for a fuller treatment of Du Bois' personal faith. Kahn engages Blum and Maribel Manning in an argument about Du Bois' status as a Christian convert. Kahn concludes that Du Bois was not a Christian in the conventional sense, as a devotee to a historical definition of the faith, and he was not an atheist or agnostic as other Du Bois scholars have mistakenly claimed. Du Bois, as Kahn perceives him, was a pragmatic religious naturalist.

12   Du Bois, *Darkwater*, 1.

13   Blum, *W.E.B. Du Bois*, 29.

14   Du Bois, *Darkwater*, 1.

15   Blum, *W.E.B. Du Bois*, 157.

16   See W.E.B. Du Bois, "Satterlee," *Horizon* 1 (1907): 4–5.

17   Blum, *W.E.B. Du Bois*, 158.

18   The story was originally published as "Jesus Christ in Georgia" but was reprinted in *Darkwater*, placing Jesus in Texas, corresponding to lynchings in both states. See Blum, *W.E.B. Du Bois*, 157.

19 Du Bois, *Darkwater*, 70.
20 Du Bois, *Darkwater*, 70.
21 Du Bois, *Darkwater*, 70.
22 Du Bois, *Darkwater*, 71.
23 Du Bois, *Darkwater*, 70.
24 Du Bois, *Darkwater*, 72.
25 DBWE 12:371.
26 Jesus' encounter with the rector is obviously based on the words of Jesus recorded in Matthew 7:21-23: "Not everyone who calls out to me, 'Lord! Lord!' will enter the Kingdom of Heaven. Only those who actually do the will of my Father in heaven will enter. On judgment day many will say to me, 'Lord! Lord! We prophesied in your name and cast out demons in your name and performed many miracles in your name.' But I will reply, 'I never knew you. Get away from me, you who break God's laws.'" See Du Bois, *Darkwater*, 73.
27 The encounter between Jesus and the escaped convict is a combination of biblical encounters. It hints at the parable of the compassionate Samaritan in Luke 10:30-37, as Jesus takes notice of him and tends to his needs, and it soon turns toward the encounter with the thief on the cross in Luke 23:39-43.
28 Du Bois, *Darkwater*, 74.
29 Du Bois, *Darkwater*, 77.
30 Du Bois, *Darkwater*, 77.
31 Kahn uses this phrase to describe a series of short stories that Du Bois wrote between 1900 and 1935 that appeared in various publications in which he depicts Jesus in a contemporary setting of the racist south, experiencing the treatment of blacks who are lynched. See Kahn, *Divine Discontent*, 108.
32 This is also an interpretation of Jesus that Howard Thurman made popular. See Thurman and Harding, *Jesus and the Disinherited*.
33 The theme of Jesus' blackness became widely known in the emergence of black liberation theology and the work of Dr. James Cone. But the theme clearly did not start there. Cone described Jesus' blackness with reference to his Jewishness. His Jewishness locates him within the context of the Exodus tradition and connects his appearance in Palestine with God's liberation of the enslaved Israelites. Cone connects Jesus' historical Jewishness with his contemporary blackness by way of Matt 25:45: "Truly I say to you, as you did it not to one of the least of these, you did it not to me." Hence, to say that Christ is black is to say that black people are God's contemporary poor and oppressed people whom Christ has come to liberate, and it is impossible to know Christ in America "without coming to terms with the history and culture of that people who struggled to bear witness to his name in extreme circumstances." See James H. Cone, *God of the Oppressed*, ed. H. Cone James, rev. ed. (Maryknoll, N.Y.: Orbis Books, 1997), 125.
34 Claude McKay, *Harlem Shadows: The Poems of Claude McKay* (New York: Harcourt, Brace, 1922), 51.
35 Georgia Douglas Johnson, "Christmas Greetings," in National Urban League, *Opportunity Reader*, 38.
36 I am referring here to Douglas John Hall's description of Martin Luther's

theology of glory vs. theology of the cross and Dorothee Sölle's reference to suffering as absurd. See Douglas John Hall, *The Cross in Our Context: Jesus and the Suffering World* (Minneapolis: Fortress, 2003), 17; and Sölle, *Suffering*, 30.

37 See J. Kameron Carter, "An Unlikely Convergence: W.E.B. Du Bois, Karl Barth, and the Problem of the Imperial God-Man," *CR: The New Centennial Review* 11, no. 3 (2012): 167–224.

38 Langston Hughes, *The Collected Poems of Langston Hughes*, 1st Vintage classics ed., Vintage Classics (New York: Vintage Books, 1995), 143.

39 See Bethge, *Dietrich Bonhoeffer*, 150.

40 Countee Cullen was Du Bois' son-in-law by brief marriage to his daughter Yolande. Cullen was the "young Negro poet" and his "black Christ" that Bonhoeffer refers to eight years after his Sloane Fellowship, when he commented on the racial condition of American Christianity in his 1939 essay "Protestantism without Reformation." See Bonhoeffer, *Theological Education Underground: 1937–1949*, DBWE (Minneapolis: Fortress, 2012), 15:456–57, editors' note 48: "*The Black Christ and Other Poems* is the title of a collection of poetry by the black poet Countee Cullen (cf. *DBWE* 10:315, note 31. [See also Bonhoeffer's reading notes on "Negro Literature," *DBWE* 10:421–22, and the editor's introduction to *DBWE* 10, 30–31—VB]."

41 Countee Cullen, *The Black Christ & Other Poems*, 1st ed. (New York: Harper & Brothers, 1929), 69.

42 DBWE 10:315.

43 Cullen, *Black Christ*, 67.

44 Cullen, *Black Christ*, 77–78.

45 Cullen, *Black Christ*, 83.

46 Cullen, *Black Christ*, 84.

47 Cullen, *Black Christ*.

48 Cullen, *Black Christ*, 87.

49 Matt 26:36-46; Mark 14:32-42; Luke 22:40-46.

50 Cullen, *Black Christ*, 99.

51 Matt 27:11-26; Mark 15:2-15; Luke 23:2, 3, 18-25; John 18:29–19:16.

52 Cullen, *Black Christ*, 96.

53 Job 2:9.

54 Cullen, *Black Christ*, 103, 105.

55 See Hebrews 11:4.

56 The sermon includes an interesting interaction with the concept of opiate religion, which Bonhoeffer encountered in Harlem. His interpretation of the poor man Lazarus at the rich man's gate, Luke 16:19-31, speaks to his developed interpretation of Christ as empathic representative action, or *Stellvertretung*. See Bonhoeffer's sermon on 16:19-31. DBWE 15:443ff.

57 Cullen, *Black Christ*, 106, 107.

58 Cullen, *Black Christ*, 108.

59 DBWE 6:253.

60 DBWE 4:86.

61 DBWE 10:314.

62 Howard College is Howard University today. See DBWE 10:314.

63   Bethge, *Dietrich Bonhoeffer*, 151.
64   Bethge, *Dietrich Bonhoeffer*.
65   Bethge, *Dietrich Bonhoeffer*, 151
66   Bethge, *Dietrich Bonhoeffer*, 421.
67   C. Eric Lincoln and Lawrence H. Mamiya, *The Black Church in the African-American Experience* (Durham, N.C.: Duke University Press, 1990), 15.
68   DBWE 10:321, emphasis added.
69   Dietrich Bonhoeffer, *Ecumenical, Academic, and Pastoral Work, 1931–1932*, DBWE (Minneapolis: Fortress, 2012), 11:95.

CHAPTER FOUR

1   Ruth Zerner also recognizes that Powell's passing reference here is more than likely a reference to Dietrich Bonhoeffer. See Zerner, "Bonhoeffer's American Experiences," 270. Adam Clayton Powell, *Against the Tide: An Autobiography* (New York: R. R. Smith, 1938), 190.
2   DBWE 10:314–15.
3   See Paul Lehmann, "Paradox of Discipleship," in Zimmermann and Smith, *I Knew Dietrich Bonhoeffer*, 41.
4   See Eberhard Bethge, "Friends," in Zimmermann and Smith, *I Knew Dietrich Bonhoeffer*, 49. Bethge quotes a BBC radio interview with Paul Lehmann, conducted on March 13, 1960.
5   I am referring to a meaning-making concept that James Cone highlights as a "mental grid." Social location plays a role in our interpretation of God and God's work in the world. See Cone, *God of the Oppressed*, 48.
6   See P. Lehmann, in March 13, 1960, BBC program with E. Bethge, R. Niebuhr, F. Hildebrandt, H. L. Henriod, W. A. Visser 't Hooft, et al. (BBC archive reference: LP26507-8). In Bethge, *Dietrich Bonhoeffer*, 155–56.
7   Delores S. Williams, *Sisters in the Wilderness: The Challenge of Womanist God-Talk* (Maryknoll, N.Y.: Orbis Books, 1993), 153.
8   DBWE 10:269.
9   See DBWE 10:268n1.
10   In February, Bonhoeffer learned of the brutal lynching in Maryville, Missouri, where a black man accused of rape was, chained to a schoolhouse roof and burned to death by a lynch mob. Two months later, he learned of the case of the Scottsboro 9. See DBWE 10:29, 30. His personal notes from the spring course that he took with Henry Ward entitled "Ethical Interpretations" indicate that he also read *The Rope and the Faggot* by Walter Francis White, which was a study of lynching. See DBWE 10:429.
11   See Cecil Wayne Cone, *The Identity Crisis in Black Theology* (Nashville, Tenn.: AMEC, 1975), 14. As quoted in Williams, *Sisters in the Wilderness*, 155.
12   Cornel West and Eddie S. Glaude, *African American Religious Thought: An Anthology*, 1st ed. (Louisville, Ky.: Westminster John Knox, 2003), 42.
13   DBWE 10:293.
14   DBWE 10:269.
15   DBWE 10:315.

16   Bethge, *Dietrich Bonhoeffer*, 150.
17   Adam Clayton Powell, "The Negro North and South," sermon delivered at Immanuel Baptist Church Circa 1893–1908, Abyssinian Baptist Church Archives.
18   Wilkerson, *Warmth of Other Suns*.
19   See Wilkerson, *Warmth of Other Suns*.
20   Milton C. Sernett, *Bound for the Promised Land: African American Religion and the Great Migration*, C. Eric Lincoln Series on the Black Experience (Durham, N.C.: Duke University Press, 1997), 37.
21   Sernett, *Bound for the Promised Land*.
22   Sernett, *Bound for the Promised Land*, 39.
23   Powell, *Against the Tide*, 70.
24   Sernett, *Bound for the Promised Land*, 14.
25   Carter Godwin Woodson, *A Century of Negro Migration* (Mineola, N.Y.: Dover, 2002), 173. Wilkerson also creatively illustrates how African American migrants attached religious significance to their move north. See Wilkerson, *Warmth of Other Suns*.
26   See Monroe N. Work, *Negro Year Book, 1918–1919, An Annual Encyclopedia of the Negro* (Tuskegee, Ala.: Negro Year Book, 1919), 9, as quoted in Sernett, *Bound for the Promised Land*, 60.
27   Nancy J. Weiss, *The National Urban League, 1910–1940* (New York: Oxford University Press, 1974), 94.
28   Wilkerson, *Warmth of Other Suns*, 9.
29   Woodson, *Century of Negro Migration*, 172.
30   Woodson, *Century of Negro Migration*, 173.
31   Sernett, *Bound for the Promised Land*, 45.
32   Wilkerson, *Warmth of Other Suns*, 249.
33   Isabel Wilkerson describes the racial changeover in Harlem from a neighborhood of middle-class Germans, Russians, Jews, and Irish "living in recently built brownstones" and working-class Italian immigrants in East Harlem to a neighborhood of southern black migrants. Wilkerson explains that whites formed committees like the Save Harlem Committee and the Harlem Property Owners Improvement Corporation to fight the "growing menace" and the "invasion" of "black hordes," which they understood to be the "greatest problem that Harlem has had to face." See Wilkerson, *Warmth of Other Suns*, 248; and Albert J. Raboteau, *Canaan Land: A Religious History of African Americans* (Oxford: Oxford University Press, 2001), 83.
34   Barbara Foley, *Spectres of 1919: Class and Nation in the Making of the New Negro* (Urbana: University of Illinois Press, 2003), 68–69.
35   Bonhoeffer claimed that "Negro churches are proletarian churches, perhaps the only ones in all America" (DBWE 10:315). That statement may refer to the influence of white capitalist racist ideology that was present even in poor white churches. Its presence is discernable in the racist engagement with poor blacks. Foley argues that capitalism was a political target of blacks and whites and that the New Negro movement was, originally, a radically political movement, linked in the postwar moment with global class and race struggles against imperialist and capitalist oppression. "The postwar New Negro was, in the eyes of many, an anticapitalist radical who envisioned African American

emancipation as inseparable from—if not identical with—the project of a class-conscious, multi-racial alliance." The fact that it became a primarily culture-focused arts movement overshadows this radical strain that connects the worldview of blacks in America with the international sentiment of people wrongly situated in the imperialist modern colonial framework. See Foley, *Spectres of 1919*, 69.

36 Wilkerson explains that the overwhelming numbers of black migrants to Harlem left concerned white property owners with a tough set of choices to make. They could try to maintain the whites-only policies demanded by groups of whites insistent on protecting Harlem from the black hordes. The whites-only policy was not working, however, because whites were abandoning Harlem with its new and undesirable African American habitants. Or white property owners could take advantage of the rising black demand and rent to blacks at a much higher price than they collected from whites. Wilkerson explains that white property owners chose to collect the higher rents. See Wilkerson, *Warmth of Other Suns*, 250; and Weiss, *National Urban League*, 106.

37 Powell, *Against the Tide*, 184–85.

38 Raboteau, *Canaan Land*, 82.

39 Cheryl Lynn Greenberg, *Or Does It Explode? Black Harlem in the Great Depression* (New York: Oxford University Press, 1997).

40 See Langston Hughes, Arnold Rampersad, and David Roessel, *The Collected Poems of Langston Hughes*, 1st ed. (New York: A. A. Knopf, 1994), 387ff.

41 Powell, *Against the Tide*, 67.

42 Powell, *Against the Tide*, 67.

43 Adam Clayton Powell, "The Attitude of the Negro Church toward the Southern Migration," address delivered at the Abyssinian Baptist Church, 3 p.m. Sunday, July 1, 1917, Abyssinian Baptist Church Archives.

44 Powell, "Attitude of the Negro Church toward the Southern Migration."

45 Powell, "Attitude of the Negro Church toward the Southern Migration."

46 See Booker T. Washington quoted in the *New York Age* 1912, as quoted in Sernett, *Bound for the Promised Land*, 20.

47 Powell, "Attitude of the Negro Church toward the Southern Migration."

48 Powell, *Against the Tide*, 70.

49 Edward Franklin Frazier and C. Eric Lincoln, *The Negro Church in America*, Sourcebooks in Negro History (New York: Schocken, 1974), 54.

50 Frazier and Lincoln, *Negro Church in America*, 72.

51 Gerhard Emmanuel Lenski, *Power and Privilege: A Theory of Social Stratification* (Chapel Hill: University of North Carolina Press, 1984), 87.

52 Lincoln mentions six models of dialectical tensions within a black theological construct. I am attending to only four here for my argument. The other two are the dialectic between communalism and the privatistic, and the dialectic between charismatic and bureaucratic.

53 Lincoln and Mamiya, *Black Church in the African-American Experience*, 12.

54 Lincoln and Mamiya, *Black Church in the African-American Experience*, 12.

55   Adam Clayton Powell, "The Church in Social Work," address delivered at the National Urban League Conference, Pittsburgh, Pa., Friday, October 20, 1922, Abyssinian Baptist Church Archives.

56   Powell, "Church in Social Work."

57   Weiss describes Powell as one of the small numbers of blacks on the committee who were all natives of the south, who had become pillars of New York's black professional community. Four had attended graduate school and three held graduate degrees. They were leading citizens of black New York's upper class: Adam Clayton Powell Sr., pastor of the Abyssinian Baptist Church. Weiss, *National Urban League*, 42.

58   Lincoln and Mamiya, *Black Church in the African-American Experience*, 12.

59   Lincoln and Mamiya, *Black Church in the African-American Experience*, 13.

60   Powell, *Against the Tide*, 190.

61   Powell, *Against the Tide*, 187.

62   Powell, *Against the Tide*, 190.

63   Powell, *Against the Tide*, 190.

64   Ralph Luker, *The Social Gospel in Black and White: American Racial Reform, 1885–1912*, Studies in Religion (Chapel Hill: University of North Carolina Press, 1991), 170.

65   *Green Pastures* was a Broadway show that ran for sixteen months, beginning on February 26, 1930. Richard B. Hays was famous for his role as De Lawd in the play. See Jervis Anderson, *This Was Harlem: A Cultural Portrait, 1900–1950* (New York: Farrar, Straus & Giroux, 1982), 347.

66   Adam Clayton Powell Sr., *Upon This Rock* (New York: Abyssinian Baptist Church, 1949), 29–30.

67   Powell, "Church in Social Work."

68   DBWE 10:421.

69   See Walter Rauschenbusch, *Christianizing the Social Order* (New York: Macmillan, 1919; repr. Waco, Tex.: Baylor University Press, 2010).

70   Powell, "Church in Social Work."

71   Powell, *Against the Tide*, 251.

72   DBWE 10:199.

73   Adam Clayton Powell, "Life and Service," sermon delivered at Abyssinian Baptist Church, Sunday, May 27, 1928, Abyssinian Baptist Church Archives.

74   Powell, "Life and Service."

75   Weiss, *National Urban League*, 238.

76   Greenberg, *Or Does It Explode?* 43–45.

77   Adam Clayton Powell, "A Model Church," *Watchman Examiner: A National Baptist Paper*, November 1930.

78   Powell, "Model Church."

79   Powell, "Model Church."

80   Powell, "Model Church."

81   Powell, "Model Church."

82   Powell, "Model Church."

83   DBWE 4:57.

84   Powell, "Model Church."

85   Powell, "Model Church."

86   Powell, "Model Church."
87   Powell, "Model Church."
88   Powell, "Model Church."
89   Powell, *Against the Tide*, 245.
90   Powell, *Against the Tide*, 222.
91   Powell, *Against the Tide*, 223–25.
92   Powell, *Against the Tide*, 226.
93   Powell, *Against the Tide*, 226.
94   Powell, *Against the Tide*, 226–27.
95   Powell, *Against the Tide*, 226.
96   Powell, *Against the Tide*, 246.
97   Powell, *Against the Tide*, 246.
98   This theme of Powell's theology showed up in Bonhoeffer's developed description of *theologia crucis* after 1930–1931. Christ is not hidden in what he later describes as Christian inactivity, or cheap grace, but in suffering, among the marginalized. Hence, we encounter God when we encounter someone who is suffering.
99   See Letter from Dietrich Bonhoeffer to Max Diestel, December 19, 1930, DBWE 10:265–67.
100 Powell, *Against the Tide*, 229.
101 Bonhoeffer apparently did not put this rebuke into writing. See Bethge, *Dietrich Bonhoeffer*, 441n26.
102 Powell, *Against the Tide*, 198.
103 That translated roughly to $35,000 in 2014.
104 Powell, *Against the Tide*, 199.
105 The relief bureau was opened shortly after Thanksgiving 1930 and stayed open until Easter Sunday 1931. See Powell, *Against the Tide*, 199.
106 Powell, *Against the Tide*, 199.
107 Bonhoeffer wrote home to a friend in Grunewald, Germany, during his Sloane Fellowship. Only later, after Bonhoeffer had returned home, did that friend respond. Bethge makes mention of the letter in his biography of Bonhoeffer. See Bethge, *Dietrich Bonhoeffer*, 128 and 206.
108 DBWE 10:315.
109 DBWE 11:446, 447.
110 DBWE 11:445.
111 DBWE 11:446.
112 DBWE 10:315.
113 DBWE 11:447.
114 DBWE 11:447.
115 DBWE 10:314.
116 This is in reference to a conversation that Bonhoeffer had with Horton upon returning from Church one Sunday. After Bonhoeffer's death, Horton recalled having seen Bonhoeffer in the lobby of the seminary, unusually emotional and excited. Bonhoeffer shared with Horton his excitement over the church and its members' exuberance about the gospel. See the editor's introduction to DBWE 10:31.
117 Zimmermann and Smith, *I Knew Dietrich Bonhoeffer*, 49.

CHAPTER FIVE

1   I agree with Clifford Green's observation about the end of Bonhoeffer's academic years. Green, *Bonhoeffer*, 4.

2   Because of the tremendous amount of written content from and about Bonhoeffer after his Sloane Fellowship, I am selective and brief in the material that I cover. I deduce my conclusions from historical evidence, historical probability, and Bonhoeffer's own words, as I highlight the connections between New York's Harlem Renaissance and Bonhoeffer, the Christ-centered Nazi resister.

3   Erich Eyck, *A History of the Weimar Republic* (Cambridge, Mass.: Harvard University Press, 1962), 299.

4   Eyck, *History of the Weimar Republic*, 319.

5   DBWE 11:50.

6   See letter from Dietrich Bonhoeffer to Elisabeth Zinn, January 27, 1936, in DBWE 14:134

7   DBWE 13:284–85.

8   DBWE 13:285.

9   DBWE 11:36.

10   The language of passing also calls to mind a signature book, *The Autobiography of an Ex-colored Man*, by one of Bonhoeffer's favorite authors, the Harlem Renaissance intellectual and first African American secretary of the NAACP, James Weldon Johnson. In Johnson's novel, the protagonist suffers many triumphs and hardships before deciding to pass for white and leave the difficulty of a black American existence completely behind. Bonhoeffer's letter to Sutz indicates his early efforts to translate his African American world experiences into his native German context. That effort led to him choosing, in years to come, to be a lone Christian voice of opposition to racist injustice. See James Weldon Johnson, *The Autobiography of an Ex-colored Man*, Penguin Twentieth Century Classics (New York: Penguin, 1990). Also, at Christmastime 1930, Frank Fisher gave Bonhoeffer a book of Negro spirituals compiled by Johnson. In exchange, Bonhoeffer gave Fisher Kurt Hielscher's edited volume entitled *Deutschland: Baukunst und Landschaft*. (My source for this information was Dr. Valerie Fisher, one of Frank Fisher's daughters. She was still in possession of the book when we spoke on the phone and emailed to me a scanned photograph of Bonhoeffer's signature in the book, "To Franklin Fisher—Christmas, 1930. Your Friend, Dietrich Bonhoeffer.") And as a farewell gift, his friend Paul Lehmann gave him a copy of *God's Trombones*, by Johnson. His friend's gifts seem to indicate Bonhoeffer's fondness for this author. See DBWE 10:30.

11   George M. Fredrickson claims that the notions of *Volksgeist* and *Volkstaat* as racial distinctions separating Germans and Jews were imported goods in Germany, borrowed from the racial distinctions that whites made in America: "explicit biological racism was not applied to Jews in Germany until well after it had been invoked to rationalize white American attitudes towards blacks." Fredrickson's research about race in America and Germany provides helpful insight into the different expressions of overt racism: "if Germans endowed themselves with a 'racial'

identity and then excluded others from it, Americans [whites] tended to racialize others and consider themselves simply human—citizens of the 'Universal Yankee Nation' and beneficiaries of what was promised to 'all men' by the Declaration of Independence." See Fredrickson, *Racism*, 72–73.

12   Hildebrandt and Bonhoeffer had been friends since they met in 1929 as students in a seminar with Reinhold Seeberg shortly before Bonhoeffer received his Ph.D. Hildebrandt was three years younger than Bonhoeffer but was very well versed in Luther's theology, such that he helped Bonhoeffer gain greater familiarity with Luther. Schlingensiepen tells us that Hildebrandt's father was a professor of history at the University of Berlin, and his mother came from a Jewish family. Hence Hildebrandt, one of Bonhoeffer's closest friends, was Jewish. See Schlingensiepen, *Dietrich Bonhoeffer, 1906–1945*, 60. Their Lutheran catechism, entitled "As You Believe, So You Receive," was published in *Monatsschrift für pastoraltheologie* [The Monthly Journal of Theology], 28, 1932.

13   DBWE 11:262.

14   Du Bois, *Darkwater*, 1. Adam Clayton Powell Sr. also refers to the same passage in his autobiography, shortly after referencing his racially diverse church staff that included "a German teacher in the Sunday School." Powell argues, "We are all created by one God and out of one blood." He continues, "These barriers which have been separating us must go because they are artificial and contrary to the principles of Jesus who prayed for the unity of mankind, and who declared that the second greatest commandment in the world is 'Thou shalt love thy neighbour as thyself.'" Powell, *Against the Tide*, 192–93.

15   DBWE 11:262.

16   I have not focused on Bonhoeffer's ecumenism or his peace witness here. Both of these are topics Bonhoeffer was inspired to embrace in Harlem. Because of space constraints and the enormous amount of literature that we have from Bonhoeffer, I am focusing narrowly on the racial dynamic for his interpretation of Christ.

17   Bethge, *Dietrich Bonhoeffer*, 207.

18   Bethge, *Dietrich Bonhoeffer*, 208.

19   Bethge, *Dietrich Bonhoeffer*, 223.

20   Schlingensiepen, *Dietrich Bonhoeffer, 1906–1945*, 103.

21   In addition, Bonhoeffer understood the church in Germany to have no reason for self-confidence. The church and the academy were in crisis, as Bonhoeffer saw it. See Bethge, *Dietrich Bonhoeffer*, 173. Larry Rasmussen identifies Paul Althaus, Emmanuel Hirsch, and Wilhelm Stapel among the theological faculty at the University of Berlin who actively sided with the Nazis and promoted Nazism with their theology. See the editor's introduction to DBWE 11:3.

22   Schlingensiepen, *Dietrich Bonhoeffer, 1906–1945*, 104.

23   Bethge, *Dietrich Bonhoeffer*, 226.

24   The reader will recall that Bonhoeffer was a Sunday school teacher for a group of boys at Abyssinian Baptist Church and a frequent guest at the Harlem YMCA, in addition to visiting homes several times of African American boys in Harlem, throughout the duration of his time as a lay leader at Abyssinian. See DBWE 10:314–15.

25 Bethge, *Dietrich Bonhoeffer*, 226.

26 See letter from Dietrich Bonhoeffer to Erwin Sutz, December 25, 1931, DBWE 11:76–77.

27 Bonhoeffer's ministry made a lasting impact on the "proletarian" boys in Prenzlauer Berg. Years after Bonhoeffer's death, one of his confirmands from the Wedding class, Richard Rother, recalled "pastor Bonhoeffer" renting a furnished room in the "slums of Berlin" to be near them. He gave his landlady explicit instructions to "allow us into his room in his absence," a move that exhibited such openness, intentional vulnerability, and trust toward them that Rother did not forget it. Also, Wolf-Dieter Zimmerman, a university student of Bonhoeffer's while Bonhoeffer worked with the confirmation class in Wedding, remembered Bonhoeffer allowing his role as lecturer to be impacted by the needs of his confirmands when one of them fell gravely ill: "Once he arrived fifteen or twenty minutes late for a seminar. It had never happened before, for he was always very reliable and correct. We looked at him in astonishment, but he only said: 'one of my boys is dying, and I wanted to have a last word with him. It had to be.'" See Zimmermann and Smith, *I Knew Dietrich Bonhoeffer*, 57–58, 66.

28 DBWE 12:90.

29 Schlingensiepen, *Dietrich Bonhoeffer, 1906–1945*, 108.

30 Schlingensiepen, *Dietrich Bonhoeffer, 1906–1945*, 208, 209.

31 Schlingensiepen, *Dietrich Bonhoeffer, 1906–1945*.

32 The youth club was such a success that it quickly outgrew its original building and was relocated to a larger facility in December 1932. But the club did not last for long. It was not affiliated with any particular religious, academic, or political party, and it dissolved in January 1933 with Hitler's ascension to power. See Schlingensiepen, *Dietrich Bonhoeffer, 1906–1945*, 208, 209.

33 Bethge, *Dietrich Bonhoeffer*, 227–31.

34 To be sure, Bonhoeffer paid attention to the poor in Barcelona in 1928–1929 as well. But those interactions occurred while he was still inside a German-centered worldview. His theological reasoning was taking place within a construct that he could not see until he stepped outside of it. That is what he did in Harlem. Powell's ministry occurred within a tradition that was outside Bonhoeffer's formative German social and theological worldview. I am arguing that Bonhoeffer entered into a different context and tradition in Harlem and was enabled to see and reflect on where he had come from.

35 For a description of the meaningful activities, poverty relief, and unemployment assistance offered by the Abyssinian Church Community House, see Powell's description as referenced in *Upon This Rock*, 29–30; also see Powell, *Against the Tide*, 156–66 and 199. The Charlottenburg Youth Group focused on job training courses for young people in addition to poverty relief for the unemployed. See Bethge, *Dietrich Bonhoeffer*, 229–30.

36 This is an observation that is shared by Bethge. See Bethge, *Dietrich Bonhoeffer*, 229.

37 Bethge, *Dietrich Bonhoeffer*, 231.

38 Bethge, *Dietrich Bonhoeffer*, 219.

39 DBWE 12:90.

40 DBWE 12:306.

41 Jacquelyn Grant, "Womanist Jesus and the Mutual Struggle for Liberation and on Containing God (Matthew 17:1-5 with Special Emphasis on Matthew 17:4)," *Journal of the Interdenominational Theological Center* 31, nos. 1–2 (2004): 3–33.

42 DBWE 13:22.

43 Bethge, *Dietrich Bonhoeffer*, 516.

44 I am not equating orders of creation and natural law as deviant ideologies. I am making the comparison of the use of empirical analysis in a religious worldview.

45 The Führer Principle, or leader principle, was the political, ideological, and religious foundation for strong unified leadership in Nazi Germany. See Bonhoeffer's discussion of the Führer Principle in DBWE 12:266–81. Bethge, *Dietrich Bonhoeffer*, 516.

46 See Joachim Beckmann, ed., *Kirchliches Jahrbuch für die evangelische Kirche in Deutschland, 1933–1944* (Gütersloh: C. Bertelsmann Verlag, 1948), 299–300, as quoted in Bethge, *Dietrich Bonhoeffer*, 269, emphasis added.

47 George L. Mosse, *Nazi Culture: Intellectual, Cultural and Social Life in the Third Reich*, George L. Mosse Series in Modern European Cultural and Intellectual History (Madison: University of Wisconsin Press, 2003), 243.

48 Bethge, *Dietrich Bonhoeffer*, 259.

49 See editor's introduction in Mosse, *Nazi Culture*, 242.

50 Schlingensiepen, *Dietrich Bonhoeffer, 1906–1945*, 125, explains that a close relationship between the church and state in Germany began during the Counter-Reformation and was based on the Lutheran doctrine of the two kingdoms. During that time, when Lutheran provincial churches in Germany were in danger, they had been protected by the Protestant German princes. This was the beginning of more than four-hundred years of a close relationship between them based on Luther's "doctrine of the two kingdoms." Luther's doctrine was essential as a theological structure for the arrangement, which proclaimed the responsibility of the state to uphold law and order in the kingdom of this world, as an authority established by God, and the right of the church to proclaim the kingdom of God unhindered by the state. Accordingly, the church had no right to interfere in matters of the state, and church members were legally bound to abide by the laws of the state. Conversely, the state provided the legal framework for the church to proclaim its message without government interference.

51 See DBWE 12:107-9.

52 Schlingensiepen, *Dietrich Bonhoeffer, 1906–1945*, 128.

53 Schlingensiepen, *Dietrich Bonhoeffer, 1906–1945*, 134. The Pastor's Emergency League was the rudimentary form of the Confessing Church. The Barmen Declaration and the Bethel Confession were two different confessional statements. The Bethel Confession was written primarily by Bonhoeffer and Sasse but edited by the numerous pastors within the Pastors Emergency League before its disappointing final draft emerged. The Barmen Declaration, which was the confessional statement of the

Confessing Church, was primarily written by Karl Barth. It remained
largely in the form that Barth intended.
54   The Bethel Confession was intended to be the article of faith that distin-
guished the Young Reformation movement from the German Christians.
55   DBWE 12:509. Also, See Bethge, *Dietrich Bonhoeffer*, 309.
56   Bonhoeffer was not completely alone in this. His friend and colleague
Franz Hildebrandt was also a strong advocate for the Jews.
57   Bethge, *Dietrich Bonhoeffer*, 300.
58   DBWE 12:100–101.
59   Schlingensiepen, *Dietrich Bonhoeffer, 1906–1945*, 127–28.
60   Dietrich Bonhoeffer, *Sanctorum Communio: A Theological Study of the
Sociology of the Church*, DBWE (Minneapolis: Fortress, 2009), 1:198.
61   See Bonhoeffer, "The Jewish-Christian Question As a *Status Confessionis*," in DBWE 12:372–73.
62   Many German pastors, including pastors in the Confessing Church, supported allowing congregations to decide whether they could cope with
having a Jewish Christian. Martin Niemöller supported this practice as
well. See DBWE 12:373n7.
63   The term *status confessionis* refers to items that are not considered matters of indifference but that define the very nature of Christian faith. See
DBWE 12:366n14.
64   See Bonhoeffer, "The Church and the Jewish Question," in DBWE
12:365.
65   See Tödt, Scharffenorth, and Stassen, *Authentic Faith*, 111. See 111n70,
where Tödt references the outline for a book that Bonhoeffer details
while in prison. See also Dietrich Bonhoeffer, *Letters and Papers from
Prison*, DBWE (Minneapolis: Fortress, 2010), 8:503.
66   See Tödt, Scharffenorth, and Stassen, *Authentic Faith*, 104; and DBWE
8:365.
67   Bonhoeffer is quoting from Proverbs 31:8. See DBWE 13:217.
68   DBWE 12:371.
69   Larry L. Rasmussen, *Dietrich Bonhoeffer: Reality and Resistance* (Louisville, Ky.: Westminster John Knox, 2005), 18.
70   Dietrich Bonhoeffer, *Act and Being: Transcendental Philosophy and
Ontology in Systematic Theology*, DBWE (Minneapolis: Fortress,
1996), 2:90.
71   DBWE 12:315.
72   DBWE 4:90.
73   Matt 7:12 NLT.
74   DBWE 6:248.
75   Bonhoeffer described prohibition Christians pejoratively as a "lifestyle
encompass[ing] the great political fanatics and ideologues and ultimately
even the crazy, pushy life reformers of every possible shade." See DBWE
6:248.
76   DBWE 6:48.
77   DBWE 6:49.
78   John 14:6.
79   DBWE 6:249.
80   DBWE 6:121–28.

81 DBWE 6:253–54.
82 DBWE 8:503.
83 DBWE 8:503.
84 Gerhard O. Forde and Martin Luther, *On Being a Theologian of the Cross: Reflections on Luther's Heidelberg Disputation, 1518* (Grand Rapids: Eerdmans, 1997), 72.
85 DBWE 10:354.
86 DBWE 10:365.
87 Hall, *Cross in Our Context*, 16ff.
88 DBWE 4:115–16.
89 DBWE 12:430–31.
90 Bethge, *Dietrich Bonhoeffer*, 305.
91 Bethge, *Dietrich Bonhoeffer*, 306.
92 Schlingensiepen, *Dietrich Bonhoeffer, 1906–1945*, 132.
93 DBWE 13:21.
94 DBWE 12:365–66.
95 DBWE 4:90.
96 Zerner, "Bonhoeffer's American Experiences," 269.

WORKS CITED

Adams, Frank, and Myles Horton. *Unearthing Seeds of Fire: The Idea of Highlander.* Winston-Salem, N.C.: J. F. Blair, 1975.

Ames, Eric, Marcia Klotz, and Lora Wildenthal. *Germany's Colonial Pasts.* Texts and Contexts. Lincoln: University of Nebraska Press, 2005.

Anderson, Jervis. *This Was Harlem: A Cultural Portrait, 1900–1950.* New York: Farrar, Straus & Giroux, 1982.

Barnett, Victoria. *For the Soul of the People: Prostestant Protest against Hitler.* New York: Oxford University Press, 1992.

Berg, Manfred. *Popular Justice: A History of Lynching in America.* The American Ways Series. Chicago: Ivan R. Dee, 2011.

Bethge, Eberhard. *Dietrich Bonhoeffer: A Biography.* Rev. ed. Minneapolis: Fortress, 2000.

Blum, Edward J. *W.E.B. Du Bois: American Prophet.* Politics and Culture in Modern America. Philadelphia: University of Pennsylvania Press, 2007.

Bonhoeffer, Dietrich. *Act and Being: Transcendental Philosophy and Ontology in Systematic Theology.* English ed. *Dietrich Bonhoeffer Works* 2. Minneapolis: Fortress, 1996.

———. *Barcelona, Berlin, New York: 1928–1931.* English ed. *Dietrich Bonhoeffer Works* 10. Minneapolis: Fortress, 2008.

———. *Berlin: 1932–1933*. English ed. *Dietrich Bonhoeffer Works* 12. Minneapolis: Fortress, 2009.

———. *Discipleship*. English ed. *Dietrich Bonhoeffer Works* 4. Minneapolis: Fortress, 2003.

———. *Ecumenical, Academic, and Pastoral Work, 1931–1932*. English ed. *Dietrich Bonhoeffer Works* 11. Minneapolis: Fortress, 2012.

———. *Ethics*. English ed. *Dietrich Bonhoeffer Works* 6. Minneapolis: Fortress, 2005.

———. *Letters and Papers from Prison*. English ed. *Dietrich Bonhoeffer Works* 8. Minneapolis: Fortress, 2010.

———. *London, 1933–1935*. English ed. *Dietrich Bonhoeffer Works* 13. Minneapolis: Fortress, 2007.

———. *Sanctorum Communio: A Theological Study of the Sociology of the Church*, English ed. *Dietrich Bonhoeffer Works* 1. Minneapolis: Fortress, 2009.

———. *Theological Education at Finkenwalde, 1935–1937*. English ed. *Dietrich Bonhoeffer Works* 14. Minneapolis: Fortress, 2013.

———. *Theological Education Underground, 1937–1940*. English ed. *Dietrich Bonhoeffer Works* 15. Minneapolis: Fortress, 2012.

———. *The Young Bonhoeffer*. English ed. *Dietrich Bonhoeffer Works* 9. Minneapolis: Fortress, 2002.

Cameron, James. *A Time of Terror*. Milwaukee, Wis.: TD Publications, 1982.

Carter, J. Kameron. "An Unlikely Convergence: W.E.B. Du Bois, Karl Barth, and the Problem of the Imperial God-Man." *CR: The New Centennial Review* 11, no. 3 (2012): 167–224.

Cone, Cecil Wayne. *The Identity Crisis in Black Theology*. Nashville, Tenn.: AMEC, 1975.

Cone, James H. *The Cross and the Lynching Tree*. Maryknoll, N.Y.: Orbis Books, 2011.

———. *God of the Oppressed*. Edited by H. Cone James. Rev. ed. Maryknoll, N.Y.: Orbis Books, 1997.

Cullen, Countee. *The Black Christ & Other Poems*. 1st ed. New York: Harper & Brothers, 1929.

De Gruchy, John W. *The Cambridge Companion to Dietrich Bonhoeffer*. Cambridge Companions to Religion. Cambridge: Cambridge University Press, 1999.

Dejonge, Michael P. *Bonhoeffer's Theological Formation: Berlin, Barth, and Protestant Theology*. Oxford: Oxford University Press, 2012.

Deutsch, Karl Wolfgang. *Nationalism and Social Communication: An Inquiry into the Foundations of Nationality*. 2nd ed. Cambridge, Mass.: MIT Press, 1966.

Dorrien, Gary J. *The Making of American Liberal Theology: Imagining Progressive Religion, 1805–1900*. 1st ed. Louisville, Ky.: Westminster John Knox, 2001.

Du Bois, W.E.B. *Darkwater: Voices from within the Veil*. Dover Thrift Editions. Mineola, N.Y.: Dover, 1999.

———. *The Souls of Black Folk*. Bantam classic ed. New York: Bantam, 1989.

———. "Satterlee." *Horizon* 1 (1907): 4–5.

Eyck, Erich. *A History of the Weimar Republic*. Cambridge, Mass.: Harvard University Press, 1962.

Fallin, Wilson. *The African American Church in Birmingham, Alabama, 1815–1963: A Shelter in the Storm*. Studies in African American History and Culture. New York: Garland, 1997.

Foley, Barbara. *Spectres of 1919: Class and Nation in the Making of the New Negro*. Urbana: University of Illinois Press, 2003.

Forde, Gerhard O., and Martin Luther. *On Being a Theologian of the Cross: Reflections on Luther's Heidelberg Disputation, 1518*. Grand Rapids: Eerdmans, 1997.

Frazier, Edward Franklin, and C. Eric Lincoln. *The Negro Church in America*. Sourcebooks in Negro History. New York: Schocken, 1974.

Fredrickson, George M. *Racism: A Short History*. Princeton, N.J.: Princeton University Press, 2002.

Friedrichsmeyer, Sara, Sara Lennox, and Susanne Zantop. *The Imperialist Imagination: German Colonialism and Its Legacy*. Social History, Popular Culture, and Politics in Germany. Ann Arbor: University of Michigan Press, 1998.

Furman, Richard. "Defense of Slavery." In *Exploring the Christian Heritage: A Reader in History and Theology*, edited by C. Douglas Weaver, Rady Roldán-Figueroa, and Brandon Frick, 154–57. Waco, Tex.: Baylor University Press, 2012.

Gates, Henry Louis, Evelyn Brooks Higginbotham, and American Council of Learned Societies. *Harlem Renaissance Lives from the African American National Biography*. Oxford: Oxford University Press, 2009.

Gilroy, Paul. *The Black Atlantic: Modernity and Double Consciousness*. Cambridge, Mass.: Harvard University Press, 1993.

Gladden, Washington. *Applied Christianity: Moral Aspects of Social Questions*. Boston: Houghton Riverside Press, 1899.

Grant, Jacquelyn. "Womanist Jesus and the Mutual Struggle for Liberation and on Containing God (Matthew 17:1-5 with Special Emphasis on Matthew 17:4)." *Journal of the Interdenominational Theological Center* 31, nos. 1–2 (2004): 3–33.

Green, Clifford J. *Bonhoeffer: A Theology of Sociality.* Rev. ed. Grand Rapids: Eerdmans, 1999.

Greenberg, Cheryl Lynn. *Or Does It Explode? Black Harlem in the Great Depression.* New York: Oxford University Press, 1997.

Guzder, Deena. *Divine Rebels: American Christian Activists for Social Justice.* Chicago: Lawrence Hill Books, 2011.

Hall, Douglas John. *The Cross in Our Context: Jesus and the Suffering World.* Minneapolis: Fortress, 2003.

Hartman, Saidiya V. *Scenes of Subjection: Terror, Slavery, and Self-Making in Nineteenth-Century America.* New York: Oxford University Press, 1999.

Hoffman, Martin L. *Empathy and Moral Development: Implications for Caring and Justice.* Cambridge: Cambridge University Press, 2000.

Huggins, Nathan Irvin. *Harlem Renaissance.* London: Oxford University Press, 1973.

Hughes, Langston. *The Collected Poems of Langston Hughes.* 1st Vintage Classics ed. New York: Vintage Books, 1995.

Jennings, Willie James. *The Christian Imagination: Theology and the Origins of Race.* New Haven, Conn.: Yale University Press, 2010.

Johnson, James Weldon. *The Autobiography of an Ex-colored Man.* Penguin Twentieth Century Classics. New York: Penguin, 1990.

———. *Black Manhattan.* New York: Knopf, 1930.

Johnson, James Weldon, J. Rosamond Johnson, and Lawrence Brown. *The Books of American Negro Spirituals: Including the Book of American Negro Spirituals and the Second Book of Negro Spirituals.* New York: Da Capo, 1977.

Kahn, Jonathon Samuel. *Divine Discontent: The Religious Imagination of W.E.B. Du Bois.* Oxford: Oxford University Press, 2009.

Lasserre, Jean. *War and the Gospel.* Scottdale, Pa.: Herald, 1962.

Lenski, Gerhard Emmanuel. *Power and Privilege: A Theory of Social Stratification.* Chapel Hill: University of North Carolina Press, 1984.

Lewis, David L. *W.E.B. Du Bois: Biography of a Race, 1868–1919.* 1st ed. New York: H. Holt, 1993.

Lincoln, C. Eric, and Lawrence H. Mamiya. *The Black Church in the African-American Experience.* Durham, N.C.: Duke University Press, 1990.

Locke, Alain LeRoy. *The New Negro: An Interpretation*. New York: Johnson, 1968.

Luker, Ralph. *The Social Gospel in Black and White: American Racial Reform, 1885–1912*. Studies in Religion. Chapel Hill: University of North Carolina Press, 1991.

Madison, James H. *A Lynching in the Heartland: Race and Memory in America*. 1st ed. New York: Palgrave, 2001.

McKay, Claude. *Harlem Shadows: The Poems of Claude McKay*. New York: Harcourt, Brace, 1922.

Mignolo, Walter. *The Idea of Latin America*. Blackwell Manifestos. Malden, Mass.: Blackwell, 2005.

Mosse, George L. *Nazi Culture: Intellectual, Cultural and Social Life in the Third Reich*. George L. Mosse Series in Modern European Cultural and Intellectual History. Madison: University of Wisconsin Press, 2003.

National Urban League. *The Opportunity Reader: Stories, Poetry, and Essays from the Urban League's "Opportunity" Magazine*. Modern Library Harlem Renaissance. New York: Modern Library, 1999.

Pfeifer, Hans. "Learning Faith and Ethical Commitment in the Context of Spiritual Training Groups: Consequenses of Dietrich Bonhoeffer's Post Doctoral Year in New York City 1930/31." *Dietrich Bonhoeffer Jahrbuch 3 / Dietrich Bonhoeffer Yearbook* 3, (2007/2008): 251–70.

Powell, Adam Clayton, Sr. *Against the Tide: An Autobiography*. New York: R. R. Smith, 1938.

———. "The Attitude of the Negro Church toward the Southern Migration." Address delivered at the Abyssinian Baptist Church, 3pm Sunday, July 1, 1917. Abyssinian Baptist Church Archives.

———. "The Church in Social Work." Address delivered at the National Urban League Conference, Pittsburgh, Pa., Friday, October 20, 1922. Abyssinian Baptist Church Archives.

———. "Life and Service." Sermon delivered at Abyssinian Baptist Church, Sunday, May 27, 1928. Abyssinian Baptist Church Archives.

———. "A Model Church." *Watchman Examiner: A National Baptist Paper*. November 1930.

———. "The Negro North and South." Sermon delivered at Immanuel Baptist Church Circa 1893–1908. Abyssinian Baptist Church Archives.

_____. *Upon This Rock*. New York: Abyssinian Baptist Church, 1949.

Raboteau, Albert J. *Canaan Land: A Religious History of African Americans*. Oxford: Oxford University Press, 2001.

Rasmussen, Larry L. *Dietrich Bonhoeffer: Reality and Resistance.* Louisville, Ky.: Westminster John Knox, 2005.

Rauschenbusch, Walter. *Christianizing the Social Order.* New York: Macmillan, 1919. Reprint, Waco, Tex.: Baylor University Press, 2010.

Richardson, Lisa. "Going Back to Find Lavinia." *LA Times,* January 16, 2000, http://articles.latimes.com/2000/jan/16/news/mn-54631/7.

Rivers, Larry O. "Our God Is Marching On: James Hudson and the Theological Foundation of the Civil Rights Movement." Ph.D. diss., Vanderbilt University, 2010.

Rumscheidt, M., ed. *Adolf von Harnack: Liberal Theology at Its Height.* London: Collins, 1989.

Said, Edward W. *Orientalism.* 25th anniversary ed. New York: Vintage, 2003.

Schlingensiepen, Ferdinand. *Dietrich Bonhoeffer, 1906–1945: Martyr, Thinker, Man of Resistance.* London: T&T Clark, 2010.

Schweiger, Beth Barton. *Religion in the American South: Protestants and Others in History and Culture.* Chapel Hill: University of North Carolina Press, 2003.

Sernett, Milton C. *Bound for the Promised Land: African American Religion and the Great Migration.* C. Eric Lincoln Series on the Black Experience. Durham, N.C.: Duke University Press, 1997.

Sölle, Dorothee. *Suffering.* Philadelphia: Fortress, 1975.

Stassen, Glen Harold. *A Thicker Jesus: Incarnational Discipleship in a Secular Age.* Louisville, Ky.: Westminster John Knox, 2012.

Stephens, Michelle Ann. *Black Empire: The Masculine Global Imaginary of Caribbean Intellectuals in the United States, 1914–1962.* New Americanists. Durham, N.C.: Duke University Press, 2005.

Thurman, Howard, and Vincent Harding. *Jesus and the Disinherited.* Boston: Beacon, 1996.

Tödt, Heinz Eduard, Ernst-Albert Scharffenorth, and Glen Harold Stassen. *Authentic Faith: Bonhoeffer's Theological Ethics in Context.* English ed. Grand Rapids: Eerdmans, 2007.

Washington, Booker T., Fannie Barrier Williams, and Norman Barton Wood. *A New Negro for a New Century: An Accurate and Up-to-Date Record of the Upward Struggles of the Negro Race.* Chicago: American, 1900.

Weiss, Nancy J. *The National Urban League, 1910–1940.* New York: Oxford University Press, 1974.

West, Cornel, and Eddie S. Glaude. *African American Religious Thought: An Anthology.* 1st ed. Louisville, Ky.: Westminster John Knox, 2003.

Wilkerson, Isabel. *The Warmth of Other Suns: The Epic Story of America's Great Migration*. 1st ed. New York: Random House, 2010.

Williams, Delores S. *Sisters in the Wilderness: The Challenge of Womanist God-Talk*. Maryknoll, N.Y.: Orbis Books, 1993.

Woodson, Carter Godwin. *A Century of Negro Migration*. Mineola, N.Y.: Dover, 2002.

Zamir, Shamoon. *The Cambridge Companion to W.E.B. Du Bois*. Cambridge Companions to American Studies. Cambridge: Cambridge University Press, 2008.

Zerner, Ruth. "Dietrich Bonhoeffer's American Experiences: People, Letters, and Papers from Union Seminary." *Union Seminary Quarterly Review* 31, no. 4 (1976): 268.

Zimmermann, Wolf-Dieter, and Ronald Gregor Smith. *I Knew Dietrich Bonhoeffer*. 1st ed. New York: Harper & Row, 1966.

INDEX